The Pov
Montgomeryshire
Village Book

THE VILLAGES OF BRITAIN SERIES

Other counties in this series include

Avon*
Bedfordshire*
Berkshire*
Buckinghamshire*
Cambridgeshire*
Dorset
Essex*
Gloucestershire*
Hampshire
Herefordshire*
Hertfordshire*
Kent
Leicestershire*
Middlesex*

Northamptonshire*
Nottinghamshire*
Oxfordshire
Shropshire*
Somerset*
Staffordshire*
Suffolk
Surrey
East Sussex
West Sussex
Warwickshire*
West Midlands*
Wiltshire
Worcestershire*

*Published in conjunction with County Federations of Women's Institutes

The Powys Montgomeryshire Village Book

Compiled by the Powys Montgomeryshire
Federation of Women's Institutes
from notes and illustrations sent
by Institutes in the County

Published jointly by
Countryside Books, Newbury
and the P-MFWI, Montgomery

First published 1989
© Powys Montgomeryshire Federation of Women's Institutes 1989

All rights reserved. No reproduction
permitted without the prior
permission of the publishers:

Countryside Books
3 Catherine Road
Newbury, Berkshire

ISBN 1 85306 053 4

Cover photograph of Montgomery
taken by Janet & Colin Bord

Produced through MRM Associates, Reading
Typeset by Acorn Bookwork, Salisbury
Printed in England by J. W. Arrowsmith Ltd., Bristol

Foreword

Tre Faldwyn, as the Welsh call Montgomeryshire, took that name from Baldwin, lieutenant to William the Conqueror. Another Norman, Roger de Montgomery, who became earl of Shrewsbury, later gave it his name.

Montgomeryshire is a county of great contrasts, from the fertile Severn valley in the east via soft rolling mountains to the low lying coast lands in the west. There are many castles and forts – especially in the east. Our county is full of secret places and hidden surprises. We find visitors return again and again to savour its attractions. Welsh is the predominant language in the west but has faded along the English Border.

Towns are few and not large. Montgomery is the county town; Welshpool and Newtown both house council administrative offices and there are three smaller but delightful boroughs – Llanidloes, Llanfyllin and Machynlleth. But life long ago was based on small settlements. These are the villages of today – depicted here by people who know them well.

It is appropriate that we are launching our book during the year in which the County Federation celebrates its 70th anniversary.

My warmest thanks to the Institutes who have willingly contributed towards its compilation and especially to Mrs Joan Shaw for editing the scripts.

Finally, please enjoy our hamlets, villages and towns described in the following pages, but above all the visual glories of the 'Paradise of Wales'.

Margery E Richards
County Federation Chairman

Acknowledgements

The Powys Montgomeryshire Federation of Women's Institutes would like to thank all those members, their families and friends, including many local historians, who have worked so hard to research and provide information and illustrations for this book. A special thank you to Joan Shaw who co-ordinated the project.

Powis Castle, Welshpool

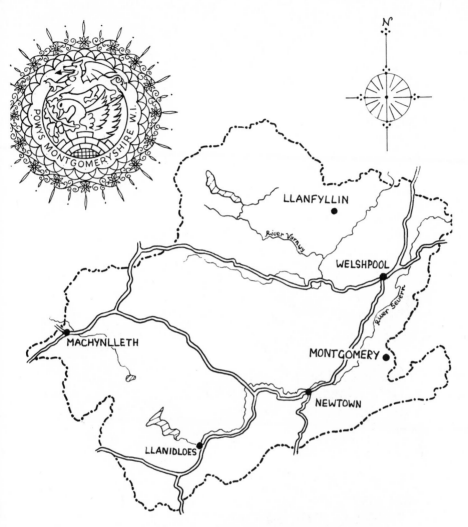

N

LLANFYLLIN

River Vyrnwy

WELSHPOOL

River Severn

MACHYNLLETH

MONTGOMERY

NEWTOWN

LLANIDLOES

County of POWYS
MONTGOMERYSHIRE

The road to Wales, Llanymynech

Aberbechan 🌿

Aberbechan is a small hamlet situated west of Abermule. As the name indicates it is 'the mouth of the Bechan river', where it joins the river Severn. The Bechan is a small, tumbling river with its source about seven miles up the valley at Gwgia Lake.

A few yards above the confluence of the rivers the Montgomery Canal passes over this small tributary in an aqueduct. It is near this point that most of the scattered inhabitants live. It was not until 1913 that these dwellings were owner-occupied, previously they belonged to the Gregynog estate.

The Montgomery Canal, part of the Shropshire Union Canal, was built 200 years ago. Until the 1930s Aberbechan wharf was a centre of activity. Canal boats delivered corn, coal, leather and limestone. The lime-kilns were adjacent to the wharf and were in use until the canal traffic ceased. The site is now home to a thriving plant hire business.

Bordering the wharf is Min-y-fron, previously known as the fulling mill. Flannel was made here, and processes including cleansing and stretching the material were also carried out. This building is now a pottery.

Aberbechan Hall is a large brick house overlooking the valley. Before the 1870s a Tudor mansion stood on the site. It was demolished but some of the oak timbers were salvaged and used as features in the new house. Rowland Fernyhough, the international show-jumper, was born and brought up here.

Further up the road is a row of derelict cottages known as Refel. These once housed four families. From about 1930 until 1960 it was one residence and included a shop which sold almost everything and served a wide area.

Continuing the journey, one comes to Pant, a three-storeyed house, some of it dating back to the 18th century, and once used as a school. An azalea planted in the garden in 1884 still blooms.

Opposite Pant is the mill. Up to the 1930s farmers took their corn there to be ground. The mill race, powered with Bechan water, drove a wheel for this purpose. Nowadays, the house and mill have been made into a pleasant residence.

Beside the mill stands Aberbechan Presbyterian Church of Wales. This small building, with a capacity of only 100, was built with the help of donations and collections in 1888, on land given by Lord Sudeley of Gregynog. In 1988 a grand centenary service was held.

Little Aberbechan, overlooking this chapel, is the oldest house in the area – black and white, dating from the 16th century. It has been well preserved and recently an inside wall of oak panelling and a small portion consisting of oak laths and wattle and daub was uncovered.

The only farm which was not owned by the Gregynog estate was Neuaddfraith, which stands on the hill over-looking both rivers. In 1865 it was sold to a wealthy industrialist from the Midlands, Mr Edward Elwell. He made farm buildings and tools, and his name can still be seen on these around the countryside. Not content with the old stone house that existed, he pulled it down and erected the typically Victorian house which stands on the site today.

Although it has only a small, scattered population, Aber-bechan is a busy place, as it is a convenient distance from the expanding town of Newtown.

Aberhafesp ☙

The parish takes its name from the brook which flows into the river Severn below the church. 'Aber', meaning mouth of the river; 'haf', meaning summer and 'hesb', meaning dried up or barren, becomes Aberhafesp – the mouth of the summer-dry brook.

In common with many Welsh names which retain their literal translations the name Aberhafesp has not been greatly changed by mispronunciation and the passage of time. It was Aberafth in 1254, Aberhaves in 1520, Aberhafais in 1592, Aberhawes in 1645 and Aber-haf-hesp in 1697.

According to a report of 1847 the population of the parish was 535. Today it is under 400.

The parish is pear-shaped, situated between Newtown and Caersws, north of the A489 road. There is no main village, but the parish can be divided roughly into six areas. There is Bwlchyffridd to the north, and, to the south the school and community centre. Towards the east lies the Pentre and Hillcrest community. In the north-west is the Bethel chapel area and in the east the Rhydyfelin chapel area. East from the school is Disquilfa Lane, the name of which means a look-out.

St Gwynog's church lies in the south-east of the parish. There has been a church here since the 12th century and a large yew tree west of the tower has been estimated to be over 800 years old. The tree has watched Aberhafesp church develop through the centuries from a primitive timber building with a thatched roof – and is still watching!

At Bwychyffridd there is a Congregational chapel, built in 1800 on a site which was formerly a ring where crowds met to watch cock-fighting and other cruel sports. 'So they took the ground from under Satan's feet and consecrated it to the Lord'. The membership increased and ten years later the chapel had to be enlarged.

The present Congregational chapel at Bethel was originally a branch of the one at Bwychyffridd and was built in 1909. Previously, there had been a small chapel which was used principally as a Sunday school. Now there is no minister at either Bwychyffridd or Bethel, but fortunately the Rev

11

Robert Michel lives in the area and runs the Sunday school at Bethel as well as helping with services at both chapels.

Rhydyfelin Baptist chapel was built in 1791, but there is evidence of an earlier church. The dissenter Henry Williams of Scafell was connected with it and there are two secret doors to be seen in the present chapel, through which dissenters could escape if they were threatened.

In 1802 the earliest school in the parish was held in the new chapel at Bwlchyffridd. There was also a school in the church gallery in 1826, which was limited to the education of 20 children, who could attend for one year only if there were others waiting for admission. At about this time there was an arrangement by which the school was held in the parish church during the summer and at Bwlchyffridd during the winter. In 1838 the Rev Richard John Davies gave a piece of land at Disquilfa on which a new school was built. At one time there were 90 children attending, taught in two small classrooms.

The present school, on a different site, was opened in 1909. It was greeted as 'A new era for Aberhafesp' by the *Montgomeryshire Express*. In 1979 the new community centre, attached to the school, was opened and in 1988 tennis and netball courts, a playing field and a children's play area were added. Of course, this is the main centre of activity in the parish.

For many years the local Young Farmers' Club has excelled in music and drama, winning the National Award for Entertainment in 1985, and winning the choir competition for three consecutive years. Rhydyfelin chapel choir is also well known, giving concerts over a wide area.

Aberhafesp Hall is situated near the church, a large brick mansion, now, sadly, divided into four dwellings. The former gardens and shrubbery are the site for about 25 houses, built since the 1960s. There is reputed to be a ghost – a lady in white who walks from the church to the east door of the hall!

Near Disquilfa Lane there is a hill where wild daffodils grow – a truly beautiful sight in spring.

At Melinygloch are the remains of quite extensive lead mining. Three levels were driven in a north-easterly direction. The most southerly contains water, and was used as a water supply so it was not explored. The middle level is blocked, while the third connects with a shaft on the hillside above. In about 1868 the Melinygloch Lead Mining Company was formed to search for lead, under the sponsorship of Lord Joicey of Gregynog Hall. It proved unsuccessful and was abandoned a few years later. Lord Joicey was deceived into investing money in a non-profitable mine. When it was known that he was due to visit the mine the miners would buy lead ore from the Van Mine, near Llanidloes, put it in the level and continue blasting. Lord Joicey, seeing the lead ore mixed with rock, would be encouraged to invest more money in the project.

Farming is still the main occupation in the parish, but there has been an increase in the numbers who travel to work in Newtown and surrounding areas. Some villagers work in the Laura Ashley factories at Newtown and Carno.

This scattered parish now has no shop – the one in Bwlchyffridd closed in about 1938, and there is no public house, though in the last century there were two in Bwylchyffridd. Now the post office has also been lost, established, again in Bwylchyffridd, since 1897. However, despite losing these amenities, Aberhafesp continues to be a thriving and close-knit community and a very pleasant place to live.

Aberhosan ᘔ🌿

Aberhosan, in the parish of Penegoes 100 years ago had no church, one chapel, a village shop, a village school and a vigorous village life. Once folk might not see each other for weeks, but the village grapevine worked as well as a modern telephone – good news, bad news, all was grist to the mill of everyday life.

The village nestles in the folds of the hills with just one road into it, but its many footpaths and farm tracks made the links that drew people together. All made their living from the land. Anyone who had no land of his own worked someone else's or gave a service to enable the work to be carried out, and each knew the value of his own contribution. The daily tasks varied but slightly and the season dictated them, so high days and holidays were made to be enjoyed.

Penbontpren, the little house at the bottom of the village, was the meeting place for children, where they would congregate to have their dinner – the forerunner of the school canteen, though each brought their own sandwiches. In summer a treat would be a grand picnic trek to Foel Madian.

If a child passed the scholarship to the grammar school in town his life changed, because he would have to lodge in town during the week, coming home at weekends. It was too far to walk or cycle each day and motorised transport was a rarity. It is different now, of course, as the building of the community school at Glantwymyn has meant the end of Aberhosan school.

The village shop lasted longer and, combined as it was with the post office, became an important place where one could buy a bit of everything. Formerly, there were two shops, the one at the top of the village also selling meat. Clothes for special occasions, or anything out of the ordinary, could be ordered from the packman who made the rounds regularly calling at each house and farm. He accepted payment in small amounts and was the equivalent of modern-day mail order services. Indeed, the regular visits by the postman serve as a valuable link in the present day.

On Sundays the chapel was the focus of village life, serving almost as a community centre. On Sunday only essential work was done, no playing, no sewing, no knitting, no frivolous reading and everyone in best clothes. Tea was sumptuous with several kinds of cake and, if one was good, no having to eat up bread and butter first! Early each summer would come the Sunday school trip. What excitement, a charabanc to take everyone to Aberystwyth, a day to look forward to and a day to look back on.

The wireless opened up the world, but village life did not change much. Television took longer to arrive, because the hills restricted the signal. The motor car brought the biggest change and Aberhosan was moving. Moving indeed – motorised farming meant fewer jobs and young people moved away. People could commute to town or even further for work and shopping. The village was changing.

Its agricultural roots remain strong, however. Aberhosan show still brings the community together and while it flourishes Aberhosan will stay on the map.

Abermule ✿

Abermule is situated four miles from Newtown and nestles in a narrow valley at the confluence of the river Severn and the river Mule.

To the north of the village stands Dolforwyn Castle, Dolforwyn meaning 'the maid's meadow'. The castle was built by Llewelyn the Last in 1273, partly as a challenge to the castle erected by the English at Montgomery, but also to keep an eye on the Princes of Powys. It was destroyed by Edward I in 1277 and by 1398 the castle, which had been roughly built, was a total ruin. During recent years there has been an archaeological dig there.

Below the castle, legend says, the beautiful Princess Sabrina was pushed into the river by soldiers on the order of her

15

enraged stepmother. She did not drown, but became goddess of the river, which is named after her. In Latin it is Sabrina, in Welsh, Hafren and in English, Severn. Milton's *Comus* describes this legend.

On the east bank of the Severn are the mutilated remains of a motte and bailey castle.

Much of the land near Abermule, and the village itself, used to belong to the monks of Strata Florida, Cardiganshire. In the *Brut y Tywysogion* it says that Meredydd ap Robert gave to the abbey of Strata Florida extensive lands and properties including The Court near Abermule, Brynderwen, Dolforwyn, Abermule Inn, the hamlet of Abermule and a fulling mill in Dolforwyn. Later the Pryce family of Newtown Hall obtained their property by lease from the monks of Strata Florida and land around Abermule formed part of their estate, covering 266 acres in Llanmerewig parish.

The chief farm in Abermule would then have been The Court and it is likely that the abbot or his steward would come there to mete out justice. Today The Court is owned by Powys County Council.

The flat land between the Mule and Cilgwrgan was originally a swamp covered with alders and willows, which was drained, cleared and brought into cultivation by Dr John Lloyd.

In 1263 there was war between the English King Henry III and Llewelyn ap Gruffydd. John Strange the Younger, who was then bailiff at Montgomery Castle, set out during the night with a large army across Kerry and Cedewain and carried off immense amounts of booty, with which he returned to Montgomery. When the Welsh heard, they pursued and killed the English – over 1,200, between those who fell in the field and those slain at The Barn, Abermule. In 1892 bones were found under the nave in Llanmerewig church.

The village evolved with the building of the Cambrian Railway in 1862. Abermule was also the starting point of the three mile single track railway to Kerry along the Dingle, a narrow gorge through which the Mule flows and which is rich in flora and fauna. It was opened in 1863 and had two halts en route, Fron Fraith and Goitre. This line carried passengers, Kerry Hill sheep to auctions, timber and brick. In 1931 it was closed to passengers and was finally closed to all traffic in 1955. Abermule station closed in 1963, under the Beeching axe, and is now used as a road haulage depot.

On 26th January 1921 there was a head-on collision of two passenger trains on the Cambrian line, when the stopping train from Whitchurch was scheduled to cross with the Aberystwyth to Manchester express shortly before noon at Abermule. Both engine drivers were killed as well as 13 passengers, including Lord Herbert Vane-Tempest, a director of the Cambrian Railway Company.

In 1892 the western branch of the Montgomery Canal was opened, chiefly through the efforts of William Pugh of Brynllywarch.

Among the notable houses in the district is Cilgwrgan – Gwrgant's Retreat – a beautiful specimen of a black and white timbered house. Another, Castell Forwyn, was built by the Rev John Lloyd in 1867 and remained in the Lloyd family until 1947 when it became a youth hostel. In 1952 it reverted to a private residence. The avenue of limes up the drive is protected.

At one time there were five water-mills beside the Mule and the Kerry railway line, some of them flannel mills, the others corn. There was also a sawmill in the village beside the Severn.

The Wesleyan Methodists used to meet in the room next to the Old Factory. Moriah Calvinistic Methodist chapel was built on Jews Common in 1862 under the direction of Mr W. R. Thomas, the village blacksmith, who laid the foundation stone.

A dame school was held at The Old Rectory, and later the

children went to Dolforwyn Church of England school. The church school, with teacher's house, was built in 1855 on a site given by the Earl of Powis. The last church service was held in 1976. The school, now a private home, was closed in 1951 when Ysgol Dolforwyn and the community centre opened.

In 1821 Brynderwen Bridge became a county bridge. It was then timber built and stood until 1852 when it was washed away by floods. It was rebuilt the same year 300 yards upstream, the second iron bridge built in Montgomeryshire.

Captain's Bridge, at the bottom of Captain's Pitch, was so named because 'the Captain's ghost' is reputed to be seen there on horseback at midnight.

Today the village has two public houses and Dolforwyn Hotel, once the rectory for Bettws church, as well as a post office and well-stocked shop and two garages. A small industrial estate has developed around the old railway station, there is a garden centre, and a caravan park is sited on Smithy Field, where there used to be a lime-kiln.

The primary school has 73 pupils, a headmaster and two assistants and ancillary staff. Welsh is taught and a percentage of pupils come from outside the school's natural catchment area. The community centre is well used by twelve affiliated bodies and a multi-purpose playing pitch is being considered.

The population is 525, but is on the brink of a development explosion, with the installation of a sewage plant. Then the village will probably become a dormitory area for Newtown and Welshpool.

Adfa 🌿

Outside Adfa's Calvinistic Methodist chapel, built in 1790, is a memorial to Lewis Evans, founder of the Methodist cause in Adfa. He was born in Trefeglwys, but while still a lad, came to live with his grandparents in the area. He was converted when 20 years old and learned to read the Bible when attending school in Llanwyddelan church. He died in 1792 and was buried in nearby Llanllugan. An adult Sunday school class is held on Sunday afternoons at the chapel and evening services take place when a minister is available.

Llanwyddelan church is a mile from Adfa, built in 1865, the font being the only item remaining from an earlier church. Services are held each Sunday morning. There is also a village hall.

Adfa stands in the hills seven miles from Llanfair Caereinion and is a busy place. Several workers are employed at the garage and there is a main gas agent and tyre specialist, as well as a builder and general merchant who also has the village shop and post office. Fortunately, the village school, built in 1879, remains, staffed by a head teacher and one assistant.

Every formerly derelict farmhouse and cottage has been bought and restored, and the peace of the area is enjoyed both by newcomers and by holidaymakers at the caravan park near to the village.

Arddleen 🌿

Arddleen is situated about six miles north of Welshpool on the Manchester to Swansea trunk road, in the valley of the Severn. Its name is derived from the Welsh, meaning a flax garden.

The village was served in the past by the Montgomery section of the Shropshire Union Canal, which is now in the process of being restored to the national network. In its heyday the canal brought great prosperity to the area, transporting local Farm produce, pipes and bricks from the now derelict brickyard at nearby Pool Quay, and bringing in coal and building stone for local use. The remains of the old water-driven mill can still be seen at The Wern, now developed as a picnic area and wild life sanctuary by British Waterways.

In the mid-1970s the bypass was constructed, taking the main A483 around the outskirts of Arddleen rather than through a series of bad bends which had become a notorious accident black spot.

In recent years there has been some new housing development in the village, but this has not prevented the closure of the village shop. The only employment within the village is still agricultural. Most residents have to travel to Welshpool, Oswestry, Shrewsbury, or even further afield, to find work.

There are two places of worship in the village. The mission church is housed in the original village school building, and the Presbyterian chapel dates back to 1820.

A new school was built in 1930 with a community centre added in the early 1970s. The present school serves not just Arddleen, but many of the small surrounding villages and hamlets and has between 70 and 80 pupils.

Situated nearby the school is Trederwen House, a building of great historical interest, parts of which date back to 1616.

Near the centre of Arddleen is the village public house, the Horseshoe Inn, and the old smithy which now houses an engraving business.

Belan 🌿

One could speed south along the route of the busy A483 daily and, by failing to pause awhile to explore Belan School Lane, two and a half miles from Welshpool, would miss completely the charm of Belan school and church sheltering snugly at the foot of the hill, on the west bank of the Montgomery Canal.

Belan translates variously from the Welsh as a pound, or animal enclosure, and a 'lump' on the side of the hill! Belan and District starts at Waterloo Turn, one mile south of Welshpool. Its outer edge continues up Red Lane to Mount Farm, where the road turns and joins the Brithdir road, then follows the Borough of Welshpool boundary along the course of the Luggy brook to the river Severn. The Belan boundary then follows the river to Glanhafren, Coedydinas Farm and White House Cottages. Many local people are farmers, or rent smallholdings, while a few are still employed by Powis Castle Estates, and many work in Welshpool. Much of the land between Red Lane and Belan school is owned by Powis Estates.

Belan and District are divided into two parts by the canal. The area between the canal and the river is fertile, flat Severn valley land, liable to flooding. It provides lush pasturage for some of the best farms in the Severn valley, with their mixed and arable farming and herds of British Friesian cattle. Above the canal is the Belan, where the pastures are rougher, with wooded slopes divided by deep dingles, and scattered dwellings or small groups of houses nestling beneath the woods.

In the spring the area is alive with birdsong and a myriad of wild flowers scent the air. To stand on the hump-backed canal bridge on a sunny spring morning is a delight. To the north the river winds its way towards the Breidden and the

21

Rhallt; to the east one sees Long Mountain and Corndon, while to the south are Montgomery and the Kerry hills. Above is the beech wood and the Rhandir wood, home for many wild creatures including the badger, which has also colonised the side of the canal. Look below; the canal is a haven for aquatic life, reeds, trees, and a pair of swans guarding their nest, reflected in the still waters.

Constructed in 1795, the canal has helped to create the economic system of the area. The coal and timber trades used the canal extensively and locks and lock-keepers' houses were built at Belan and Brithdir. Limestone was transported from Llanymynech and the impressive kilns at Belan are now a picnic area. Most of the lime was used by local farms and transported by wagon. A row of cottages with black and white facing was built near the lime-kilns for canal workers and another row of stone cottages at Sarnau-bryn-caled for waggoners and Powis estate workers. The estate sawmill and timber yard were sited to take water from the canal to drive the turbines, as was Coed-y-dinas, the Earl of Powis's model farm. This was built on a grandiose scale in an attempt to 'get even' with his rival John Naylor, who applied mechanised farming extensively on his Leighton estate.

Increased population created a demand for a school, which was built by public subscription in 1840 on land donated by the Earl of Powis. It is unusual in that it was built to be used as both school and church, the chancel being added in 1868. Stone was brought from Welshpool and Strata Marcella Abbey, north of Welshpool, by canal and horse and cart. The 3rd Earl, Viscount Clive, enjoyed walking along the canal to evensong, where he would read the lesson. Communion services are now held once a month, with festive gatherings at Harvest, Christmas and Easter.

Since its closure in 1985 the school building has been rented from Powis Estates. It has always been the heart of the community. Senior locals tell of dancing classes, of Saturday nights dancing to Bert Evans and his band, and of village shows with ladies chasing cockerels, skirts held high (the Belan Belles, 'Johnny Jones the Welshman' from the Malthouse called them in one of his poems!).

Belan has its share of interesting buildings and history. A pretty rose-clad pub, The Horseshoes, is the village local and nearby is the Bogeys Pool, once the terror of wayfarers. Glanhafren, formerly the fishing lodge of the Earls of Hereford, now has an otter reserve. The Cavalry fields flat beside the river were the drill ground of the Montgomeryshire Yeomanry and the field below the canal, belonging to the Moat, was used in Victorian times for steeplechasing.

A turnpike gate and cottage stands by Limekilns Lane and there is another on the Churchstoke Road, called Brandy Cottage. Rose Cottage, a pretty wattle and daub house, was a Tŷ Unnos (a dwelling built in one night). Land and farms in the area of Llwynderw ('oak grove'), particularly the Court and Wernllwyd, were once owned by Strata Marcella Abbey. Legend has it that a stone near Trehelig ('willow town') farm marks the birthplace of St Beuno, a rather malevolent saint who bewitched an oak tree so that Welshmen might pass beneath its branches unharmed, but Englishmen were struck down.

Before the road was widened the hamlet of Llwynderw was the Saturday night meeting place for the young people of the area, who came to the shop and gathered about the oak tree which was then at the bottom of the hall drive.

Belan does not live in the past. Farms are highly mechanised with modern methods of farming. Tourists are catered for in style and there is a small light aircraft field at Trehelig with plans for a helipad. Many derelict houses have been restored and the community revitalised. All this, together with the proposed opening of the canal to navigation, augurs well for the future.

Berriew

About AD 600 a Prince of Powys gave the township of Aberriw to St Beuno to establish a church. Set in an oval churchyard, the church is situated near a natural crossing of the river Rhiw, from which the name of the village – Aberriw, the mouth of the Rhiw – is derived. The modern Anglicised form, Berriew, only dates back to about 1750. St Beuno travelled from Berriew all over North Wales, where there are more churches dedicated to him than to any other saint.

The early history of Berriew was dominated by the ford of Rhydwhiman across the Severn, near its confluence with the Rhiw. Kings of England and Princes of Wales, or their representatives, met there frequently to debate problems and make treaties. There was a great battle near the ford in 1257, when Llewelyn ap Gruffydd, Prince of Wales, scattered a combination of English lords and the lord of Powys. A major treaty between Llewelyn and Henry III was signed at the ford in 1267.

The modern village and parish dates back to Tudor–Stuart times, when many of the picturesque black and white houses were built. The village was a centre for the wool trade, fleeces being brought from the hills for sorting and sale in the market hall. The prosperity of the village has at many periods rested on the backs of the sheep in an area of good agricultural land where the value of lime was early recognised.

A second period of building took place during the Napoleonic Wars when the land near the Severn produced good corn crops. Almost all of the present village centre dates back to one or other of these building periods, presenting a picture of architectural beauty.

During the Civil War, Berriew was firmly on the side of Parliament. A reforming tradition has continued, with edu-

The old smithy, Berriew

cation a source of enlightenment and of division. A free school was established by the will of Humphrey Jones of Garthmyl in 1655, and it produced a number of striking individuals. One of these, an illegitimate boy called Thomas Jones (1756–1807) proceeded from Berriew school to Shrewsbury school and thence to Trinity College, Cambridge. There he was Senior Wrangler and Head Tutor and he played a significant part in the modernisation of the university, being regarded as one of the outstanding characters in its history. His legitimate half-brothers David and William Owen were also mathematicians of note at the same college.

Another reforming character from Berriew was Dr Edward Johnes (1773–1846), notable for his support of the Chartists, who sought electoral and other reforms in the early 19th century. His son, Arthur James Johnes (1808–1871), became a famous judge, while his grandson, Arthur Charles Humphreys-Owen (1836–1905), was noted for his zeal in promoting education both locally and nationally.

During the Civil War, the main house in the parish, Vaynor (Y Faenor) was occupied by George Devereux, a relative of the Earl of Essex, the Parliamentary Commander. His grandson and great-grandson became the 9th and 10th Viscounts of Hereford, the premier viscounts of England. When the 10th Viscount died in 1748 without an heir, the title moved away from Vaynor. Another family took control of the estate, whose descendant today is Colonel John Lyon Corbett-Winder, Lord Lieutenant of Powys from 1974 to 1986.

While the fortunes of the village have been based mainly on agriculture, the community has always been well served by local craftsmen – coopers, carpenters, builders, painters, glaziers, shoemakers, smiths, saddlers and so on. It is still notable for a number of such craftsmen, including an excellent local baker. Berriew is fortunate in that its everyday needs are well catered for by grocers, a butcher, a newsagent and post office. It also has its share of inns and public houses, including one reputed to date back to the 14th century, two from the 17th century and another only a little, if at all, later.

As might be expected from its educational tradition and reforming sons, the church – represented by the parish church of St Beuno, two mission churches and the chapels, both Presbyterian and Methodist (and including one very old Wesleyan chapel, built in 1797) – has always played a big part in community life. It still does, with an ecumenical tradition now well established.

Apart from the church groups, the community is well served by organisations ranging from the Brownies to a Darby and Joan club. There is a thriving Young Farmers' Club of great value to the community and its young people make a useful contribution to the Best Kept Village competition, in which Berriew has had outstanding success with firsts in Montgomeryshire, Powys and Wales. The activities of all these organisations are chronicled in the monthly Berriew

Newsletter, produced by volunteers and distributed free to all households in the community.

Apart from its own architectural beauty, the village gains much from the sparkling river, crossed by a beautiful bridge, recently restored, and by its setting in a circle of wooded hills. Berriew's beauty has in part, perhaps, led to several visits from the Royal Family, culminating in the walk-about by Queen Elizabeth II in 1986, now commemorated by a plaque on the post office wall.

The village is celebrated in a poem by one of its older residents:

'Enfolded by the ever-changing hills,
Graced by the church beneath its shading trees,
Companioned by the river's flow, which fills
With ever garrulous melody, the breeze,
In clusters of black and white the village stands,
Timeless, serene, among the verdant lands.'

Bettws Cedewain ✣

Bettws Cedewain probably derives its name from the Welsh 'Betws', meaning a prayer house, or bead house, where the number of prayers repeated were recorded on a rosary of beads. This place of worship was situated in the parish of Cedewain.

It lies in a sheltered valley on the banks of the river Bechan, a tributary of the Severn, with Newtown five miles to the south and Welshpool ten miles to the north-east, the nearest markets and shopping centres.

Through the centuries the village has grown around this crossing of the ways over the river, probably used by Roman soldiers, and around the ancient church founded by St Beuno in the 6th century. The church contains what is believed to be

The New Inn, Bettws

the only pre-Reformation memorial brass in the county, dedicated to the memory of the Rev John ap Meredyth, 1531, for his work in planning the building of the tower. The organ, given to Bettws by Lord Sudeley in 1872, has a mechanical player attachment with three rolls of chants and hymns.

In the belfry tower could be found the first schoolroom in Bettws, probably approached in those days by a wooden ladder. It must have been quite exciting for those first scholars, clambering up to this little room in their boots or clogs. Eventually the pupils moved from their belfry to quarters specially built for them in the churchyard and were taught there from 1852 to 1896. Then the new building, used to this day, was opened across the river, with clergy and banner bearers leading the procession from church to new school.

The building has been modernised and pupils have the added facilities of the community hall, opened in 1985.

Many old farms and houses have survived and still stand in good condition. Until 1914 most of the properties in the area belonged to the Gregynog estate, but a large portion was sold then by Lord Joicey and many more were sold by the Gregynog Estates Company in 1920, with first preference given to sitting tenants. Amongst them were some beautiful black and white houses. Glanbechan has the date 1651 carved on the gable end. Highgate, mentioned in Domesday records in the 11th century, is a large timber-framed farmhouse where the hounds of the estate were once kept, and Pontyperchyll has a panel decorated with the Tudor rose.

Some buildings have been converted for different purposes through the years. Of four inns only the New Inn remains as such. Cwmcignant is a farmhouse, the Talbot has closed as an inn and the Red Lion has become the picturesque general stores and post office. The old mills, the smithy, the tailor's shop, the old post office, the wheelwright's and the cobbler's have all been converted for private use or closed.

When the site for the Presbyterian chapel in the centre of the village was purchased in 1823 there were two cottages on the plot. These were moved wholesale to the back of the site with the aid of jacks, rollers, horses and a team of strong Bettws men. One of the cottages has been modernised and still peeps from behind the chapel; it is named 'Hideaway'! This chapel provided a more central meeting place for services previously held at the Glomen and other farms in the district.

From 1920 more and more houses were built, so that with the Brynteg estate, Cae'r Nant and the recent addition of Ffordd Newydd, the village extends in a wide semi-circle to the south and west. One of the private houses, Heulfron, built to the north of the church, is on the site of the almshouses in which the Weaver Charity made provision for eight needy people from Tregynon and Bettws. The occupants had to be of good character and had to obey a curfew – 'Every almsperson must be withindoors and the outer door locked by 9 pm under penalty of 1s fine'. Harsh treatment on a summer's evening!

Farms have seen great changes. Now most are run by one or two members of a family and few employ extra labour on a regular basis. One of the greatest changes must be from the long-drawn-out hay and corn harvests to the quicker methods of silage making, baling and combine harvesting.

Modern gadgets make the role of the farmer's wife different, too. She is now more involved in the running of the farm, has her own business in connection with holiday accommodation, or undertakes employment away from the farm. The old custom of her rearing poultry to provide housekeeping money is no longer feasible, unless done on a large scale.

Reduction in the size of families in the last century is evident when today's census is compared with that of 100 years ago. Today's population totals approximately 400, compared with 579 last century, despite the increasing size of the village.

However, development has meant a great demand for recreational facilities. In 1981 it was decided that a new hall was needed to replace the prefabricated one erected in 1921. What a terrific community spirit fund raising engendered! Barbecues, raft races, sales, concerts and log chops brought money rolling in, so that the necessary funds had been raised when the new hall opened in June 1985. It is now a real task to find a free evening there. What a contrast to shove ha'penny in Bettws Hall yard and ball throwing against the north wall of the church – some of the earlier pastimes!

Beulah

Today's housewives in Beulah, near Llanidloes, get into their cars and go down to the supermarket for their weekly shopping. Not so the Beulah housewives of days gone by. Yes, there was a weekly shopping trip, but it entailed a good hour's walk to catch the 'two' train at Glanyrafon Halt to travel to 'Llani', a mere three miles away. The goods they needed were tea and sugar, cheese and maybe a special piece of meat for the Sunday roast. They would return, loaded for the 'five' train. Then there was the uphill walk to arrive home by seven o'clock.

Flour, of course, was obtained the hard way. Sacks of corn were carried by horse to Cenarth Mill for milling, with probably another journey to collect the flour the next day.

Beulah chapel has the date 1877 above the door, and not far away, at Blaenglyn, is reputed to be the site of one of the earliest Baptist chapels, though there is nothing there now but a yew tree. Before the chapel was built the earlier meeting place was at Garthfarw Farm, where the present-day dining room with its high ceiling and pew-shaped alcoves by the fireplace, gives an aura of the old chapel.

Calvinistic Methodists met at nearby Lodge Farm to listen to the wise sermons of Hywel Harris.

There are still many glorious walks, climbs and sights to see. One of those, which would have to be searched for, is the 100 ft waterfall of Treflogaufach. If one still has energy to climb, because climb one must to reach the top of Pegwns Poll, the reward on a clear day is a view of Rhayader Mast and the Elan valley.

There has never been a bus service in Beulah and children used to walk over three miles to school carrying packed lunches, no school dinners then! For as many as 60 children there were only two teachers, and a special potato-picking holiday was a bonus today's children know nothing about.

Brooks 🌿

A somewhat scattered village, nine miles from Welshpool and eight from Newtown, Brooks consists mainly of farms, forming a truly agricultural community. These farms are now mainly given over to livestock, and the introduction of milk quotas has meant that some have ceased to be dairy farms. There are a few private houses and one holiday home.

The Old Smithy is now a flourishing craft centre, producing silver and pewter photograph frames and specially designed jewellery, giving employment to several local people.

Fortunately the village has retained its own post office and shop but the school, which was built to replace the old church school, was itself closed in 1965 when attendance was reduced to eight pupils and one teacher. It is now a community centre used for public functions and club meetings. Younger children now attend Berriew primary school and the older ones go to Welshpool high school.

The Anglican church, built in 1857 in Ride Wood, combined a school with church functions but was demolished in 1969, the school having ceased to exist long before. Now the only place of worship is the Presbyterian chapel, opened in 1872 and renovated in 1907.

The first chapel was in a barn at the Rock in 1820, but this moved in 1823 to a cottage called Tynycoed and services were held there for nearly 50 years. The remains of this chapel are still visible opposite Stingwern.

An ancient camp at Ucheldre is listed as an ancient monument.

Originally the name of Brooks was Brookland. This name appears in the conveyance by Mrs Bridget Devereux under which certain lands in 'Brookland' were left to the church-wardens of Berriew church, the income from which was to provide bread for poor of the parish. This is now part of the Berriew Relief in Need charity.

Some difficulty is experienced in the management of village affairs because the village is in two parishes, the centre in Berriew and the chapel area in Bettws.

Buttington 🌿

Buttington lies on the main Shrewsbury–Welshpool road. The railway nearby carries a good inter-city service between Aberystwyth and London, and the Shropshire Union Canal, the river Severn and Offa's Dyke, which runs to the side of the church, are all close by.

The canal has recently been opened for pleasure craft, and the Heulwen, or Sunshine, boat regularly takes handicapped children for summer cruises, starting from Buttington wharf.

Plans are in hand for a new road from Buttington Cross to Middletown because of heavy summer traffic, some of which pauses to visit the Moors Collection of rare poultry and animals.

Employment is mainly in agriculture, but there is also a productive brickworks making bricks and tiles and employing some 50 people.

The oldest house is Garbetts Hall. A de la Garbette came over with William the Conqueror and was given 'a parcel of land on the slopes of the Long Mountain'. He later shortened his name to Garbett.

A map of 1635 shows a piece of land called Nelly Andrews Green. A farm is still called by that name, supposedly haunted by Nelly's ghost! The green was the site of a celebration of dances, but who Nelly was remains a mystery.

The parish church is built on the site of the battle of Buttington, AD 935. The font and west window are from the old Cistercian abbey of Strata Marcella. The monks from this abbey owned land on the Long Mountain and some of the place names are reminiscent of this, for example, Monks-field, Paradise Cottage and Lord's Building. The monks were sheep farmers and the wool was brought to the river at Pool Quay.

During the building of the school several pits containing human bones were discovered.

The Buttington and District Amateur Operatic Society puts on a musical each November, which is always popular, and the Cantore Choir performs oratorios in the spring.

Bwlch-y-Cibau ✿

The name of the village means 'valley of the acorns' or, more poetically, 'the pass of the acorn cups'. It lies north of the A495, a few miles west of Llansantffraid.

The parklands of the two nearby country houses, Bryn-gwyn Hall and Brynderwen Hall, hold varied species of fine trees. There would have been ideal feeding grounds in the oak woods for the herds of pigs formerly driven through the valley.

Dominating the village is Christ Church, designed by the eminent architect Sir Gilbert Scott and built in about 1863. Nearby stands the school, closed in 1967 and now the focus and meeting place for village life.

During the Second World War evacuees from the cities were welcomed to the school. Then coal fires were the only means of heating the lofty building – no lighting, apart from the flickering flames, for story reading. Mains water was unheard of, cold water being supplied by a rotary pump. At break, pupils hastened over the muddy, stony playground to the toilets, which were not very inviting when the wind blew from a certain direction!

Frequently gas mask drill was practised. At the sound of the headmaster's whistle everyone donned masks and hurried to a less vulnerable place – a wet ditch in the field over Cefn road. Every pupil was accounted for on return in a damp and muddy state.

On freezing winter days the enormous steaming pan of milk on the smoking fire signalled lunchtime. How the smoky-flavoured drink with black specks was relished!

One evacuee, billeted with an elderly couple, had never seen farm animals before. He lifted the cow's tail in a pump-like action, thinking that was how the milk came. Forty years later he revisited the area to thank the school and the villagers for their kindness.

Bwlch had a strong Home Guard and on one occasion German planes dropped incendiary bombs on the wooded area around the village.

'Postman Pat' vans now chug along the lanes, a far cry from the postman of former years, who sorted the mail at the village post office (now closed) at 6 am, then set off on Shanks' pony over hill and dale. His visit with letters and snippets of local gossip was eagerly awaited. On Christmas morning Mr Owen, one-time postman, possessor of a fine tenor voice, would sing a Welsh carol to herald in the festival.

Older residents recall many tales about local characters. One was the village carrier – with donkey and cart – Tommy Banker, Plas-y-Nant, so called because of his imaginary bank account! Another was Betty Price, who has a lane named after her.

Near the school a tenement once existed which sheltered a notorious family of coin-clippers, believed to be capable of any crime.

But that was long ago, now more respectable residents have left their mark. Parry Thomas, for instance, the celebrated but ill-fated racing driver, was the son of the vicar. His giant car *Babs*, crashed on Pendine Sands in 1927 as a new world record was attempted and he was killed. The car was buried in the sands but, remarkably, 50 years later was on the track again, having been excavated and restored by an enthusiast.

Outwardly, the village seems to remain unchanged, but recently dwellings have been landscaped into the surroundings and new families occupying these will undoubtedly add to the vigour of village life.

As the Welsh poet Eluned Lewis wrote:

> 'We have a birthright
> No man can sell;
> And a secret joy
> No man can tell.'

Caersws ✿

Caersws, as the prefix 'Caer' signifies, was the site of a Roman camp. The suffix 'Sws' is derived from Swswen, which was the name of the 'queen' of the area at the time of the Roman occupation. Many local excavations have been carried out and some of the discoveries are to be seen in the National Museum in Cardiff. Development of any sort is forbidden in one part of the village, where the Roman camp was situated. Indeed, a new housing estate has been named Llys Rhufain, which means Roman Court.

Before the Clywedog Dam was constructed across one of the tributaries of the Severn, and a dyke built along the bank through the village, Caersws suffered from severe flooding.

Standing on the bank of the river Severn and at the junction of several fertile valleys, Caersws became an excellent centre for trading produce from the local farms. A cattle and sheep market is still held in the Smithfield. As a result of the dense sheep farming, woollen factories were built, which have now been converted into dwellings. There was a local brick-kiln, and Gwynfynydd is an example of a house built of the warm red brick.

Maesmawr Hall is a fine example of Elizabethan architecture. It is now a comfortable hotel, in beautiful grounds, catering for tourists and for social and business functions. A mansion known as The Park is also very old and Queen Elizabeth I is reputed to have slept there.

What was once a large Poor Law institution where the magistrates court was held, is now a hospital for the mentally handicapped. Much good work is done by the League of Friends.

Caersws is in the parish of Llanwnog and once had a small but busy railway junction connecting the Van lead mines with the main line. The famous Welsh poet, Ceiriog, was stationmaster for one period. Nearby was another very busy railway junction known as Moat Lane. That junction has been demolished, as the South Wales line was closed as part of the Beeching plan. Many local men worked on the railway. The village is fortunate, however, to have a good railway service, with the Aberystwyth–London trains stopping regularly.

The village is also fortunate to be within four miles of Laura Ashley's main factory at Carno, which gives employment to a great number of men and women. In addition, there is a building firm, well-known throughout the county and beyond, which is responsible for many imposing buildings such as the town hall at Newtown and the Agricultural Pavilion on the Royal Welsh Show Ground in Builth Wells. When the new school was built on the outskirts of the village the old school became six workshops, which are thriving.

Caersws has the advantage of a modern surgery and dispensary, the latter eliminating the journey to Newtown for prescriptions, several shops where all household needs are catered for, and a garage which stands in the middle of the village.

Caersws comes under the care of the Community Council, which is responsible for a population of about 1,400. There are several bungalows and flats built specifically for the elderly, who also benefit from a Meals on Wheels service when necessary.

There are many organisations for the villagers to join, with a large village hall for meetings, functions and indoor sports. There are two recreation grounds – one is a playing field for children, while the larger one is used for outdoor sport, including a very successful football complex for seniors and juniors.

The Church in Wales and the various chapels unite in many services during the year and support each other's causes.

Carno 🦢

The word Carno, according to legend, comes from a hill in the centre of the parish called Clorin. The word dates from Roman times and means a horse. If one stands by the old station, now part of the Laura Ashley factory, it is easy to identify the shape of the hill as the back of a horse. Farmers today still use the word in Welsh – 'tori'r glorin', the tail of a foal. Part of the village near the church is by the heel of Clorin. Since carn means hoof, one could say the village is 'ei garn o' – by the hoof of the horse.

Academics say Carno is named from the cairns which surround the village; or from the river Cerniog nearby. But local people prefer the legend!

On the approach to the village there was a blacksmith's shop and a few yards away the Black Boy Inn – where the locals wetted their whistles while waiting for their horses to be shod!

The Aleppo Merchant Hotel, formerly Ty Ucha, was re-named after his ship by a sea captain who became its landlord.

A tollgate, removed when the new road came, was the subject of an old tale. It is said that a smallholder from Talerddig, on his way home from Carno, called at the Sarn Inn. He spent all his money and, hoping to avoid his tollgate fee, he bundled his donkey onto the cart. When asked for his fee he replied, 'Ask the driver, I'm in the shafts'.

In 1700 a local boy, Evan Evans, mainly self-taught, won a scholarship to Oxford. He became rector of Christ Church, Philadelphia, USA, and there is a statue to him in that city.

The school where Evan received some education was in a loft over the church, but in 1851 a school for 30 children was built on the site where the Laura Ashley factory is today. It cost £200, raised by local subscription and parents paid 1d per week to educate a child, 1½d if there were two from one family. The idea caught on and by 1872 a school for 140 was built, costing £1,800 to be paid for from the rates. It is a Welsh school, though there is a certain amount of English with the influx of English workers to the area.

A character who became famous for wickedness and had a boyhood connection with Carno was Morris Llewelyn Humphreys, 'Murray the Humph' to his fellow rogues. The book *No Gangster so Bold* by John Morgan gives an account of his life. His father emigrated to America in the early 1890s and Morris grew up on the Chicago streets. He became right hand man to the gangster Al Capone and when Capone was imprisoned Humphreys became 'head boy'. He died in 1965 – a double millionaire. Carno does not want its good name associated with such a character, but he *was* a chip off a very sound block – Humphreys y Castell.

Superstition comes into the story of some Carno pigs which fell ill at the end of the last century. The farmer felt he must consult the crynjar, or wizard. So, as was the custom, he sent a neighbour to see the wizard, who lived at Panty-beni, Llangurig. The neighbour was given a bottle containing a piece of paper. If this was hidden in the farmer's bedroom without his knowledge, he was told, the pigs would recover. The bottle was discovered 50 years later and is now in the Welsh Folk Museum, St Fagan's, Cardiff.

But Carno is not just a place of legends and of yesterdays. With the establishment of the Laura Ashley factory and, more recently, the discovery of an illicit 'drugs factory' locally, it has been the scene of more modern history.

Plasllysun, the mansion on the village outskirts, scene of the drugs affair, was the 'home' of Carno WI from its foundation there in 1917 (Mrs Adams, occupier of The Plas was the first president) until 1922. In due course the Adams estate passed to an American, who apparently manufactured drugs in the cellars. In 1976, after extensive police work, the gang was brought to justice, and the tale was told in a book called *Operation Julie*.

It was in 1963 that a small factory making oven gloves, aprons and so on opened in Ty Brith. No one imagined this would grow into the famous Laura Ashley concern with shops worldwide. As well as being a boon to local labour the directors do their best to preserve the Welsh heritage. All their signs are in Welsh and English and all the reception staff are bilingual. Also, they keep up the old school by using it as their conference room. 'The tragedy of losing Laura herself in 1985 will be felt for a long time,' say the locals. She is buried in Carno.

Castle Caereinion

Mapped out on an ordnance survey sheet, the parish of Castle Caereinion resembles a fleece laid out to dry, the cluster of buildings making up the village being a pitch-mark on the left flank, its limbs stretching north and south. The area is one of great natural beauty, of gentle wooded slopes and green valleys interlaced with hedgerows, where flora and fauna abound.

It is an agricultural area, many of the farms belonging to the Powis Castle Estate. The majority of these depend on beef and sheep, though there are a few dairy farms and a small amount of arable land on the lower ground. Milk is collected daily by tanker and taken to Four Crosses creamery to be made into cheese.

There is constant banter among the beef and dairy sectors as to who earns the easier living and who works the longer week, though it is unlikely either would change the habits of a lifetime!

As farming intensifies, the workforce has dwindled, making way for machines doing the work in a fraction of the time. Most of the seasonal work – silaging, shearing, ploughing, combining and hedge-brushing is now done by contractors. Recently, EEC policies have encouraged sheep production, which, in turn, has led to a trend towards in-wintering sheep. This has caused the expansion of several small agricultural engineering businesses which thrive on the fabrication and erection of purpose-built sheep sheds and, to some extent, compensates for the scarcity of openings for youngsters in farming.

Diversification is fashionable in the modern agricultural world and this, together with labour-saving devices in the home, has meant that more farm housewives have taken part-time jobs away from the farm.

During the summer tourists make great use of the A458 coast road from Welshpool. Alongside it, on the narrow gauge railway, the *Llanfair Jennie* puffs between Welshpool and Llanfair Caereinion, stopping at Sylvaen, Castle Caereinion and Cyfronydd on the way, sides bursting with visitors and enthusiasts.

From the surrounding hills, where Welshmen of history kept a look-out for the threat of invasion from marauding Englishmen, one can look down on the village. St Garmon's spire stands like a sentry guarding everything. The old landmark of Dolarddyn Hall, where Henry Tudor is said to have rested on 13th August 1485 on his journey from Milford Haven to Bosworth, collecting Welsh support for his battle against Richard III, has been demolished. Nearby, where the main road and the old Llanfair road link, a new red-brick farmhouse has taken its place. So begins another chain of history.

Cottages which had fallen into dilapidation are restored and inhabited by newcomers, adding extra shades to the tapestry of country life. For instance, at the Glyn a pottery has been set up. Elsewhere a spare-time woodturner produces much admired work, and a farmer's wife has turned her hobby of dressmaking into a successful business.

Cyfronydd Hall, once the home of landed gentry, is a residential school for girls; at the old gashouse a herbalist uses remedies passed down by word of mouth from mother to daughter. At Brynhwdog is kennelled a pack of hounds which hunts regularly for the foxes which pose a threat to sheep and lambs.

The village itself resembles one from a story book. Farm, terraced cottages (aptly called The Row), shop, inn, church and school all stand within a cat's whisker of each other. But it is growing. New housing draws new young families. Many commute to towns to work, but are happy to live in a rural community. This bodes well for the future of the primary school, which now has over 40 pupils. Peripatetic teachers come to take Welsh and music, and pupils have the use of the new community hall, which the villagers worked hard to finance, aided by grants from various authorities.

Castle Caereinion is under the pastoral care of the clergy in Welshpool, and services are held at St Garmon's on three Sundays a month. During 1988 under the government's Job Creation scheme, the churchyard, which may have been the site of the motte and bailey castle from which the village derives its name, was levelled and reseeded to ease the task of upkeep. The old school, owned by the church authorities, was, under the same scheme, given a facelift and flowers planted which make the village approach colourful.

Ty'n Llan, at the entrance to the village, is one of a handful of demonstration farms in Wales. Much has been done as an experiment to see how the demands of intensive modern farming can be reconciled with the preservation of wildlife and traditional landscapes. A nature trail leads to a conservationist's paradise.

The village shop, which a newcomer was heard to remark 'stocked everything or else could advise what to use instead, or how to manage without', doubles as post office and newsagent. Should supermarkets ever gain a complete stranglehold and force the closure of such establishments, village life will be the poorer.

Another dual role is carried out at the Red Lion, where 'mine host', when not serving behind the bar, designs wedding gowns and runs a factory where his designs are made up.

There is a thriving youth club, badminton club and Women's Institute, all meeting regularly in the community hall. During the summer the bowling club plays on the Rectory Ground, and the Golfa Hill provides a splendid site for an 18 hole golf course. As autumn approaches the local concert party prepares its Christmas concert. The old year becomes history, of which all are a part. What better spot to have made history than Castle Caereinion!

Cefn Coch ✍

St Mary's church, Llanllugan, the parish church for Cefn Coch, stands above the river Rhiw, dates from 1239 and is said to have been the only convent church in Wales. On the south side is a filled-in doorway which possibly led to the cloisters. The convent itself would have been on the flatter ground nearer the river. There are signs of buildings, possibly workshops, on the north side. The east window dates from the 15th century; it has been pieced together and shows, on the left, the figure of a nun. Lewis Evans, the famous Montgomeryshire revivalist, was buried here in 1792. Services are held every Sunday and there is also a church institute.

Carmel church, two miles from Cefn Coch, was built in 1825 as a branch of Adfa chapel. Services are held here occasionally.

The village, four and a half miles from Llanfair Caereinion, has an entertainment hall attached to the hotel, popular with young people for miles around and with holidaymakers from the two nearby caravan parks. The post office opens a few hours each week.

At Red Ridge is an outdoor-pursuits centre catering for the mentally handicapped. It was opened in 1978 and stays open all year round. Activities include sailing, canoeing, Canadian canoeing, archery, pony trekking, climbing, hill walking, cross-country skiing, caving, canal cruises and visits to places of interest. The instructors are extremely experienced in working with the mentally handicapped in the context of outdoor pursuits.

Ceinws ✤

Ceinws, also shown on some maps as Esgairgeiliog, lies in the valley of the river Dulas, right on the edge of Montgomeryshire and very near to the Snowdonia National Park. The main road from Corris used to meander through the village to Machynlleth, but it now runs down the valley on the other side of the river, although the old road remains for local traffic to use. The village boasts a pub, a post office, a shop, a small housing estate, built in the mid-1950s when many of the old cottages were condemned, and a well-signposted art gallery at Plas Rhiwgwreiddyn at its southern end.

The name of Ceinws comes from one of the farms in the area. There are two possible interpretations of Esgairgeiliog. Literally, it means 'the ridge of the leg of the cockerel', but it may be a corruption of Esgair-Cyfeiliog, since the village lies on the boundary of the old Hundred or Cantref of Cyfeiliog. Esgairgeiliog was the name chosen for the station on the old light railway, but the community has also been known by other names at various times, including Aberglesyrch, from the river Glesyrch which flows into the Dulas nearby, and Achor, the name of the original Congregational chapel.

Although the family from Ceinws farm built a mill soon after 1800, the village really owes its growth to the slate industry. There is a record of slate being mined in the area as early as 1500, but the quarries flourished mainly in the second half of the 19th century. The main vein of slate lies a little to the north, but there were three 'accidental' quarries strung out along the Dulas valley. These, the Era or Colorado quarry, the Cambria Wynn quarry and the Rhiwgwreiddyn quarry, operated at various times from 1818 onwards. They were all operating in the last 30 years of the 19th century, but after 1900 production fell and despite various attempts to reopen them, the last finally closed in 1934. Slate is still mined at Aberllefenni just over a mile away. The buildings in which the slate was processed can still be seen in the centre of the village and today form a small industrial plant, making medical supplies.

A very necessary part of the slate industry was the Corris, Machynlleth and River Dovey Tramroad, which was built in 1858 to carry slate from the quarries down to the port of Derwenlas, which lay at the highest navigable point on the river Dyfi. From there it was carried by ships to provide

45

roofing slates for the houses in the new towns which were developing as a result of the Industrial Revolution. Not only was there a station at Esgairgeiliog, but, just before the station, to the south, a private tramroad forked off to the right, crossed the river and ran to the Era quarry. During the First World War, this branch line was extended for another mile in order to carry timber from the forest.

Corris lies 300 ft above Machynlleth and at first the railway worked by gravity, the trucks being pulled up by horses. It converted to steam in 1879. Originally it was intended only to carry slate, but in 1883 the passenger service became official and for a period around the turn of the century it also flourished as part of the early tourist industry. Trips along the line were widely advertised and tourists could travel from Machynlleth to Corris and then on to Tal-y-Llyn by horse bus. Passenger services closed in 1930 and the goods service came to a sudden halt in 1948 when the track deteriorated to such an extent that one morning some of the sleepers were found suspended in the air near the Dyfi Bridge! Signs of the old railway can still be seen near Ceinws and part of the old station is now a bus shelter, but, alas, only a very small section of the railway near the Corris Railway Museum to the north, has so far been restored.

After proving its worth in the First World War, the forestry industry developed, and, as the quarries finally closed, the forests grew and the workers transferred from one industry to the other. The planting of the Dyfi Forest, which has its headquarters in Ceinws, began in 1926 and this is now extremely productive.

During the 19th century, there was much religious activity in the village and feelings could run high amongst the various nonconformist groups. Today there are two large chapel buildings to bear witness to this strength of feeling – the Calvinistic Methodist Ebenezer chapel, built in 1840, and the Tabernacle, dating from 1895.

Most of the houses rise along the hillside to the east of the Dulas. Happily, not all the cottages which were declared unfit for human habitation in the 1950s were pulled down and some of them have been attractively modernised, without losing their original character. One such is Ty Isaf, which was originally built in 1790 and, appropriately, restored in 1970.

From many of the houses and cottages it is possible to see, high on the hillside to the south, one of the Cretan windmills belonging to the Centre for Alternative Technology. This was opened in 1974 in the old slate quarry at Llwyngwern, where there was another station on the Corris Railway and where quarrying stopped in 1952. It has become a major tourist attraction, bringing visitors from all over the world, and provides an absorbing day out for the family.

The Centre also serves a more serious, educational purpose for those concerned about, and involved in, exploiting renewable sources of energy. A route around the site leads to various exhibitions – demonstrations of the different ways of harnessing solar energy, the many kinds of generators which use natural resources, a conservation house which cuts heating costs to a minimum, demonstrations of organic gardening and the possibilities of water power, and a practical example of how to attract wildlife to one's garden.

A guide of 1895 described the charming scenery which excursionists on the Corris Railway could see from their 'bijou saloon carriages' as they travelled along the valley of the Dulas – the river alongside, the forests around and the mountains above. This is still the overwhelming impression as one stands in the village of Ceinws a century later.

Churchstoke ॐ

Several times the church of St Nicholas in Churchstoke has undergone restorations, the last in 1812, when the nave was rebuilt. Its parish registers, the oldest in Montgomeryshire, date from 1558. The Norman tower is the oldest part still standing and there, on the same level as the gallery, the village's first school was held from 1772–1812. In 1846 the village had only six school pupils. Now, in the latest school, built in 1965, there are between 70 and 80. The village is growing.

It stands on the Montgomeryshire–Shropshire border, where that border does eccentric twists and turns. Welshpool is nine miles away, Newtown 14 and Shrewsbury 23.

Change is rapid. A new estate and many other houses have been built recently and a number of other houses demolished to allow for road improvements.

Still standing, however, is Churchstoke Hall, which is early 17th century and Fir Court, dated 1685. On the doorstep of The Coed farmhouse is a tombstone whose Latin inscription, translated reads: 'Here is buried Richard Evans late of Brithdir, doctor of medicine died May 2nd 1701 at the age of 46'. How it came to be there no one knows!

People visit Churchstoke from miles away to shop at Harry Tuffin's supermarket. This, together with Thornhills Hatchery and farming provide the main employment in the village. There is a post office and grocery store, a newsagent and grocer, a pottery, a cafe and a nursing home. Once there were four shoemakers, three blacksmiths, two bakers and flour merchants, three grocers, two ironmongers, three millers, two maltsters, two stone masons, a cooper, butcher and harness maker. Two public houses serve the village, the Horse and Jockey and the Court House. The latter once lived up to its name, for cases were heard there and one went on to the Old Bailey.

The Wesleyan chapel was first built in Coed Lane in 1855 and held services there for 20 years, after which a new one was built in Blue Bell Road.

Activities are varied and include a widely known and popular amateur dramatic society. Its W.I. is very active. In 1985 they staged a two-day event depicting Churchstoke down the years.

Coedway, Crew Green, Bausley & Criggion ✤

The four villages are strung along the B4393 as it enters Wales.

Approached from Prince's Oak, a landmark on the border of England and Wales, Coedway comes first. Its name means 'The way through the wood'. Formerly it had a blacksmith's shop, a cobbler's, baker's, the Old Hand and Diamond Inn and a garage. Now only the last two remain.

There is a Presbyterian Church of Wales chapel, which was built in 1865. Inside is a pipe organ presented by Hamar Davies in 1898. Prior to that music was provided by a string orchestra. A Mr G. Pryce Wynne played there for 60 years. At the manse next to the chapel there was once a minister who christened his sons and daughter after the rivers – Hafren, Tanat and Deva.

A schoolteacher, Miss Kathleen Derwas, was the proud possessor of one of the first Austin Seven cars in 1920.

Crew Green, further along the road, saw its biggest change when the railway closed down and the track was made into a road in 1956. This must have changed life for many residents, because, prior to that date the only way to Melverley and beyond was either by a precarious walk over the bridge with only the railway sleepers between walkers and the river,

49

which regularly flooded, or by taking the road to Four Crosses and Llanymynech. The old station cottage still exists.

The post office closed in the late 1970s and the garage in 1987. Once a week for many years a surgery has been held in the village, either in a cottage, the Fir Tree Inn or, as now, in a farmhouse. Where now modern houses stand at Bryn Mawr there was, years ago, a brickworks. The village also had a smithy, but all that remains is the name on the cottage door.

Bausley, dating back to the 11th century, had many names before settling to its present one. The Primitive Methodist chapel was built in 1875 and is still in use every Sunday. The 38 council houses at Bryn Hafren were built after the Second World War and a school and community centre followed in 1961. Before the school was built children of the area walked to Alberbury or Llandrinio.

Criggion, in the shadow of the Breidden Hills, has been written about by Canon A. C. Roberts in his book *Between the Rock and the River*. Rodney's Pillar, on top of the Breidden, is the local landmark, built probably to commemorate Admiral Rodney, whose fleet in the 18th century was built largely of local timber. On a visit to the pillar while staying at Criggion vicarage, Cardinal J. H. Newman was inspired to write his most famous hymn *Praise to the Holiest in the height, And in the Depth be praise*.

The quarry in the area started in 1911 with six men and in 1988 employed 40. Prisoners of war were employed there during the Second World War. A radio station was opened in 1942, receiving and transmitting all over the world.

The village hall, built in 1950 is very much in use. The village has always had its own post office. It has been moved from one cottage to another, but now serves a wider community than previously because other post offices in the area have closed. Criggion is practically a privately owned estate, so there have been few changes.

Many 'characters' have lived around the area, but there is only one ghost – a black dog at Criggion Hall.

The characters included a couple called Black Poll and Jack who, around 1910, would sell periodicals for pennies one week and then beg them back the next to sell to other keen readers. Bill 'Bullock' Lloyd frequented local hostelries and sold everything they wanted from the two baskets he carried, and Bill Titley was a well known 'milestone inspector' in summer, who spent the winters in Llanfyllin workhouse.

It is believed certain local gentry in days gone by formed a society called the Breiddenites, who met every year for a celebration meal. Another event still remembered by a few of the older villagers was the 'wake' in which Criggion would join with Alberbury – a village just over the English border – on the first Sunday after 10th October, a goose being part of the feast. After the First World War there was a Peace Rejoicing in a tent after church service.

Darowen

Darowen is thought to mean 'Owain's oaks', and Owain Glyndwr's army, stationed in Machynlleth, may well have sought refuge in the surrounding hills. However, the origins of this small hill village, which stands a little over 600 ft above sea level, are probably very ancient.

The area around Darowen was an important site in pre-Christian days, and three standing stones, of which two remain, marked a 'Noddfa' or sanctuary within which the village was situated. A large standing stone (over 6 ft high) stands square to the points of the compass in a field known as Cae yr hen eglwys ('old church field') to the south near Tal y Wern, while a smaller stone (just under 4 ft high) can be found to the north of the village in a field just below Cefn

Coch Uchaf. The third stone (Carreg y Noddfa), to the east at Cwm Bychan Mawr, was blasted apart for stones in 1860. In times past, suspected wrongdoers were given a head start in a race to the stone and if not caught were allowed to go free.

It is notable that the two remaining stones lie on a line which passes through the site of the church. The line has an accurate bearing on one of the Five Heads of Plynlimon above Bwlch Gwyn (White Gorge), which in turn is in direct line with Carn Gwilym, at 1,852 ft, which faces the breast of Plynlimon Fawr. The Darowen stones would seem to be part of a system of pointer stones which are spread around the moors of Plynlimon, and Darowen may have been a place of considerable significance at the time of the Wessex Culture around 2000 BC.

The church of St Tudur, founded in the 7th century, has a circular churchyard which suggests an ancient site. The saint is assumed to be buried there, and his feast day on 15th October used to be marked by a young man being carried aloft round the parish on his companions' shoulders while others beat him with sticks. In 1864 a crumbling 14th century church was replaced by the present one at a cost of £667.0.9½d. The register of baptisms, marriages and burials dates back to 1633, and the chalice, still in use, to 1575. A pleasant place to visit or worship in, services are held each Sunday at 2 pm in the Welsh language. The church is widely known in the area for its Plygain, traditionally an early morning Christmas service, now held on an evening in January.

The Methodist chapel, founded in 1823, was in regular use until its closure in a dilapidated state in December 1987. Originally services were held at the nearby farm of Tynllwyn.

The old school in the centre of the village was opened in 1841 and enlarged in 1871 to accommodate 100 pupils from as far afield as Abercegir, Tal y Wern and Cwm Bychan.

Waiting at the gate, Darowen

When it closed in 1971 the roll was down to 12. The school building was used frequently as a community centre until the end of the 1970s and was the venue for many parish events, including lively Christmas parties with blazing log fires, and the celebration of the Queen's Silver Jubilee in 1977. It is rarely used now and is in a poor state of repair.

The Old Rectory is a handsome building, and a number of the small terraced cottages in the village have been attractively restored. The Cefn, once the Red Lion Inn, now offers bed and breakfast.

In the 18th century when the population was at its greatest and lead was mined locally at Cwm Bychan and transported to Aberdovey, the village supported a shop and a blacksmith in addition to the inn. Today, at the heart of a busy farming community, and with a population of around 30, Darowen is a lively and industrious place. There are three thriving businesses – a builder, an agricultural machinery maintenance specialist, and a small publisher. In August it is not unusual for the population to double when holidaymakers fill cottages now considered too cramped for modern day dwellings.

Fron Goch, the prominent hill in the lee of which the village lies, rises to 930 ft and provides a wonderful panorama of the surrounding countryside. Remains of the walls of a Romano-British hill fort are visible in the grass just below the summit. About half-way up the hill from Darowen one can see, over a field to the right, a barn beside which an old hanging tree used to stand. The tree was chopped down around 1900, but this part of the hill is still known as Bryn Crogwr or Hangman's Hill.

Darowen is fortunate in being well wooded. Native deciduous trees such as oak, ash, hazel and beech are plentiful, and there are extensive Forestry Commission plantations nearby.

Good cover is provided for many species of birds and wild animals. Foxes and badgers are frequently seen, and red kites are by no means a rarity. Performing their breathtaking aerobatics high above Fron Goch, then swooping deep into the valley below, these finest of fliers have nested in the vicinity in recent years.

Derwenlas

Once a small but busy port, the village of Derwenlas lies about two miles south-west of Machynlleth. It is on the south bank of the river Dyfi, where the river bends right into Derwenlas. The name means 'green oak', after an oak tree which grew at the entrance to the old port. Until the 1860s, when the railway was built, the port exported the products of mid-Wales. The river is tidal up to Dolgelynen, enabling tall ships to sail up at high tide.

There were three quays, Tafan Isa, Quay Ellis and Quay Ward. In 1847 500 tons of bark, 40,000 ft of timber, 15,000 oak poles, 1,500 tons of slate, and 586 tons of lead were exported. In the same year rye and wheat, 1,000 tons of coal, 2,000 tons of limestone, animal skins and hides, sugar, wine, tea, soap and powder for blasting in the lead and slate industries were amongst the imports at Derwenlas.

Ships built at Derwenlas were made of wood, which was plentiful locally. The last to be built was the *Rebecca*. The tombstone of John Evans, timber merchant of Morben Isa, stands in front of Chapel y Graig.

In spring the trees were felled and men, women and children stripped the bark with a barking chisel. This was then packed into bundles and sent to the English tanneries for the leather industry. There was also a leather industry in Machynlleth.

An early description of the road serving Derwenlas was given by John Ogilby in his road book *Britannia*, published in 1675. Although Derwenlas is not shown on his map, recent archeological excavations have confirmed the existence of a 17th century road, which later became the Machynlleth—Aberystwyth turnpike.

At Derwenlas the old road passes the Black Lion before beginning a steep climb to the 260 ft contour. This part of the old road is of particular geological interest, as it has been cut through the Derwenlas Formation of Silurian rocks, so that there is an almost uninterrupted section of the Formation visible.

An Act of Parliament of 1858 approved the construction of a tramroad of 2 ft 3 ins gauge from the Aberllefenni slate quarries in Merioneth to Morben Lower Wharf. The tramroad was to be horse-drawn throughout its length and the first train ran on 30th April 1859. However, the arrival of the standard gauge railway ensured the tramroad's early demise.

At Glan-y-Afon, Derwenlas, a section of the tramroad

survives as a length of slate-built terrace-way some 200 ft long, now converted into a raised garden. The tramroad here follows the old course of the Dyfi, before the building of the Aberystwyth–Welsh Coast railway extension caused the river to be diverted to the north.

In the village there were two public houses, the Black Lion, which still stands, and Tafan Isa, now Tan-y-ffordd, which marked the original entrance to the port. The village has three sections, Pentre Cilyn where the lime-kilns were situated; the centre, Pentre Nant, where there was a small stream, and Pentre Efail where the blacksmith's was situated.

Evidence still remains of the 'brief glory' of Derwenlas. The sloop *Milo* was sunk purposely below Llugwy to prevent the river bank from eroding and its shape could still be seen up to 1948. When the railway came in 1863–4 it took most of the traffic from the road, and the port faded. The river itself, formerly the mainstay of the old port, was diverted, and a new channel made. This is known by today's fishermen as the 'new cut'. The scar of the old river can still be seen, especially at times of wet weather when the river resumes its original course.

Dolanog

Dolanog is a very small village north-west of Welshpool and south-east of Llanwddyn on the B4382. It has a population of about 60, of whom the majority are Welsh speaking. It nestles between the hill called Allt Dolanog and the river Vyrnwy.

Dolanog is renowned for its association with the Welsh hymn writer Ann Griffiths, who died young and is buried with her two-week-old baby at nearby Llanfihangel. The Anne Griffiths Memorial Chapel is one of the principal buildings in Dolanog, stone for its building in 1904 having been quarried from a rocky outcrop near the river a few hundred yards away. Many people come to see her home, Dolwar Fach, and the chapel. To accommodate the influx of visitors, in the late 1960s the council built a sheltered car park and public conveniences.

The church, St John's, was built in the 19th century together with a vicarage, school and schoolhouse. The Church of Wales sold the vicarage as a private house in 1987. The school closed in 1945 and is now the venue for all village functions. These include whist drives, sales of work, suppers for various occasions and a monthly meeting of a ladies group called Cymdeithas y Merched.

In the centre of the village is a shop/post office, once the site of the village blacksmith's, and a garage. The car park was once a timber yard. Surrounding these are eight council houses and a few scattered private homes. Water comes from a well on the Allt and during a dry summer has to be replenished by the Severn Trent Water Authority using bulk tankers.

The name Dolanog comes from two Welsh words dol and eog which mean 'the dale of the salmon'. Every autumn there is a wonderful display of salmon trying unsuccessfully to leap the waterfall on the Vyrnwy. Reluctantly, they spawn in the gravel a little downstream. The rapid water of the fall powers a turbine which once supplied electricity for the whole village but now only provides power for the Mill Farm. Until 1986 it was the sole source of energy for St John's church.

Within less than a hundred yards of the village centre three bridges cross the turbulent Vyrnwy. The furthest is a private Bailey bridge to the Mill Farm. The other two, the ancient and modern, stand contrastingly side by side. The original stone, hump-backed bridge is so narrow that visitors never cease to wonder how large vehicles ever negotiated it. In 1984 the new stone-faced, concrete bridge was built to facilitate the passage of large modern lorries and agricultural machinery.

Most of the men in the village are self-employed in either agriculture or building, while the women who go out to work have wide-ranging occupations in Llanfair Caereinion or Welshpool.

Some farms and private homes provide accommodation for the many visitors who come to enjoy Dolanog's natural beauty and serenity. Many people fall in love with the area and holiday homes are much sought after.

Dolfor ✍

Dolfor was described in 1891 as one of the most 'comfortable parishes in the county, or, indeed, in the Principality', the chief local landowner having restored all the farmhouses on his estate and seen that the farms were 'well-managed and hedges neatly trimmed'. The village today is close-knit and friendly, careful for its inhabitants and its traditions.

It has been fortunate in its benefactors. For instance, the Free church was built in 1923 on land donated by the late Mr R. Williams of Old Court. The parish church, built in 1851, stands on land given by the Rev G. A. Cheese. When the old school of 1865 ceased to function as such it became the property of Mr E. W. W. Beddoes, a great-nephew of the original donor. He, in his turn, presented the property to the inhabitants for a village hall. The present school was opened in 1952.

The villagers repay their generous benefactors by being generous themselves and have consistently raised money to restore their churches and for local and national charities. Here the Young Farmers' Club contribution is considerable in that tradition. Their annual carol singing, which at first raised £29, in 1987 brought in over £500.

Built in the Early English style in 1851, the parish church has a nave, south porch, chancel and bell-gable. Its roof is delightful, with scissor trusses above hammer-beams supporting a trellis of diagonal ribs springing from corbels and linked by collars between trusses.

Penybryn Methodist church is the village's other place of worship. There are services most Sunday afternoons in the summer, ending with harvest thanksgiving in October.

A Christian Centre at Cefn Lea provides Christian holiday facilities – for 300 when it opened in 1979, and for 13,000 in 1988!

Girls with learning difficulties come from all parts of Great Britain to Dolfor's Camnant, a private school for girls. In 1981 a riding school was added, affiliated to the British Horse Society, which provides lessons for children from special schools in the county. There is an all-weather area and facilities for those in wheelchairs as well as the able-bodied.

Dolfor sits in the hills on the main Manchester to South Wales trunk road. Its inn was formerly a resting place for drovers and was mentioned in journals around 1590. Indeed, it is believed to have been an inn since the late 1300s. There the drovers' routes split, one going over the Kerry hills to Craven Arms, the other to Shrewsbury and the Midlands.

Two of the district's notable houses are no longer occupied. Caelydon is reputed to have once been used as a prison. Gilfach, probably 400 years old, has a massive frame, possibly of Montgomery oak, originally used as ships' timbers.

One very old cottage which has now been restored, Crugyn, is built on a slope 1,300 ft above sea level and there are other fine old dwellings. Glog Farm, two miles from the village centre, is named after the hill behind the house, which reaches a peak of 1,569 ft. On its summit are two prehistoric mounds, now under a preservation order and where ploughing is forbidden.

The village show and sports day is a splendid annual event, with something for all tastes – races, football, rounders, carnival, fell racing, tug of war, arts and crafts, cookery, disco and barn dance. The Bonfire Night firework display raises money for Dolfor school, and the sheep-dog trials attract entrants from all over Britain.

Dylife

Dylife – the place of floods – has a population of just 27, a far cry from its heyday as the centre of the lead mining industry in Wales in the mid-1800s when more than 1,200 people lived and worked in its environs. Today, the Star Inn stands sentinel, as it has for 350 years, but catering now for tourists who find their way to this wild spot on the edge of the Plynlimon escarpment. Connections with its mining past are relegated to a few faded photographs on the walls.

Legends abound here. Stories of ghosts are still told round the firesides on long winter evenings. One is of a miner killed during a cave-in. He was buried in the nearby cemetery, but his clothes were buried, as was the custom, on the hillside near to Ty Maggi. His ghost kept appearing, showing his old friends his jacket and imploring them to take it. This went on for several months until the friends decided to dig up his clothes to solve the mystery of his ghost's unrest. Duly retrieved, the jacket revealed, to the amazement of all, the miner's life savings inside. They divided the monies between themselves and the ghost was seen only once after that – smiling and waving goodbye!

Perhaps the most famous legend concerns the blacksmith of the mines whose wife suspected him of liaisons with 'camp followers'. She followed him from their home 10 miles away in Llanidloes, taking their small daughter with her, and her worst fears were realised. When she challenged him he flew into a terrible rage, murdered both wife and daughter and hurled their bodies down a deep mineshaft, which he thought was unused. But his crime was soon discovered. He was tried, found guilty and forced to make his own head and body cages and the gibbet iron. The gibbet, on Penycrogbren – Gallows Hill – to the south of the vicarage, was a grisly caution to all who passed along the old road between Staylittle and Machynlleth, as the corpse of the blacksmith slowly rotted into history. In the 1930s, some 230 years later, at the site of the old gallows, the iron head cage, with the skull inside, was unearthed. This gruesome relic is now in the Welsh Folk Museum, St Fagan's, Cardiff.

Dylife, set in remote and magnificent scenery, boasts of the Ffrwdd Fawr, one of the highest waterfalls in Wales, where Afon Twymyn cascades to the floor of the Pennant Gorge, almost 200 feet below. The dramatic vista of the gorge can be seen from the narrow mountain road from Staylittle to Machynlleth. It remains one of the finest in Wales.

Forden

Forden probably derives its name from the four fording places across the Severn within the village. It is a long, scattered village between Welshpool and Montgomery, bounded by two rivers, the Severn and the Camlad. The Camlad is the only river that rises in England and flows into Wales.

Present-day Forden is changing fast, with many new houses being built. Dairy farming has always been, and still is, the predominant industry within Forden's boundaries. One farm, called Gaer, which means a fortress, was the site of a large Roman camp.

In recent years new, small businesses have begun in the village, but a blacksmith's shop built in 1887 is still being used for its original purpose. The old railway station, closed in 1965, is now a concrete works, which makes paving slabs, drinking troughs for cattle and other items. Other businesses include the making and selling of garden furniture and there is a builder, an undertaker, an artist and an electrician. Part of Cilcewydd Mill, a large red-brick building built in 1850 as a flour mill, is today used as a car body repair shop. Also in the building is a business selling motor bicycles.

Brynhyfryd Hospital is Forden's largest employer. It was founded in 1795 as a house of correction, or workhouse. Today it cares for about 50 mentally handicapped adults and provides work for over 100 people.

The village shop/post office is still open and there are three public houses in the village – The Railway Inn, The Square and Compass and The Cock Hotel. Edderton Hall, a lovely Georgian-style mansion, once part of a large farming estate, is now an hotel and country club run by a former Shropshire Member of Parliament.

In 1972 a large purpose-built community centre was opened, providing Forden with a much-needed meeting place.

Forden school has over 45 pupils and is a Church of Wales school. A village newsletter, begun some years ago by a 15 year old schoolboy, is eagerly awaited each month by all its readers.

The parish church, St Michael's, was consecrated in 1867, the foundation stone having been laid on 19th June 1865. St Michael's has a beautiful pre-Raphaelite stained-glass window by Sir Edward Burne Jones. A Congregational chapel in the centre of the village is a few years older than the present St Michael's.

Among the headstones in St Michael's churchyard is one bearing the verse:

> Beneath this tree lies singers three,
> One tenor and two basses.
> Now they are gone it's ten to one
> If three such takes their places.

The inscription on the stone is actually in memory of two people, not three:

> In memory of John Roberts, who departed
> this life Oct 1st 1827 aged 85
> and of
> Robert Roberts, who departed this life
> March 16th 1839 aged 67

Were they father and son? Or two brothers? No one knows. The original yew tree beneath which the grave lay blew down in the early 1970s. A new tree, planted by Mr George Parry, the then churchwarden, is growing well.

Being on Offa's Dyke footpath, Forden is visited by many people who enjoy walking this long distance path. Consequently, bed and breakfast is now offered by several householders.

Forge

If all the Hughes, the Pughs, the Joneses, the Thomases, the Evanses, and others who lived here over a century ago could see Forge now, would they recognise the village and feel at home?

A backward journey was attempted as far as the memory of the oldest truly native inhabitants could go. They bridged the gap between the 'now' and the 'then', helped by a few faded photographs, yellowed maps and documents, which triggered the recall of stories heard in their long-gone childhood.

The five fulling mills, or pandy, close to the river Dulas, where their grandfathers had worked, no longer exist. The last was still in good condition in 1937 but, gradually, whatever materials could be easily removed were taken; the same fate must have befallen the other four.

The Welsh name Bontfaen, now on road signs, refers to an older and much narrower bridge than the present one.

One of the two shops used to be near the bridge, a general store and post office. The wall postbox remains. Amongst other things one could buy treacle toffee and home-brewed nettle beer. Once a month its owner went to Machynlleth to give her order to a commercial traveller for goods which came from Liverpool. She would memorise the daily transactions, afterwards written in her ledger by a local lad. That shop closed in 1927.

The other was across the bridge, opposite Rose Cottage. A newcomer, who bought her 200 year old cottage in 1962, remembers the ham bought just before breakfast from Mrs Jones the Shop. She also recalls her new neighbours saying, 'How nice to see a little girl in the village'.

Families with six or more children were not unusual in the early 1900s. Photographs of the time show this; smiles fixed for ever and, in their best clothes, farmers, shepherds, foresters, their wives and children stand in front of the chapel built in 1872. A full congregation meant 60 to 70 people and three services every Sunday. Now the numbers vary between three and nine. A christening which took place in 1988 was the first for many years.

'No doubt about it, being a child in those days was very different from today,' said one old inhabitant. 'We were only three when we went to school and walked over the footbridge, Pont y Plas, it's gone now.' A sigh. 'Our mother, lunchtime, met us halfway to Penegoes with a can of hot soup.'

'We were not allowed to speak Welsh, punished we were if

we did.' 'Remember the bakehouses? We had two in the village. Everyone helped with collecting wood for the ovens and baking was done on a rota system.'

From communal cooking to wells. One which never dried up was condemned in 1956 after a local boy caught polio. Mains water came to Forge soon after. 'Easier than lugging buckets, but well water was sweeter.'

'When did you stop using oil lamps?' Surprise. In 1931 Forge had its very own small power station by Dolgau Farm. Dai the Electric set it up. Soon after the first wireless, with big valves, came to Ty Croes. It is now at Plas y Forge, where its owner moved to.

Many remember the fire at the Dolgau power station just before the 1937 Eisteddfod. And at Plas y Forge one can see the medal presented in 1925 to D. Evans for rescuing sheep from the water-filled slate quarry near the bridge – deep beyond measure they say.

Until 1939 there were 22 houses on the left bank and only Plas y Forge on the right, alone since 1640. By the late 1960s nine more houses had joined them, including Nant y Arian, so called because of the silver coins washed to ward off the plague. In 1980 there was building on both banks, and now there are 40 dwellings.

Forge has been known for years by the beekeeping fraternity because Alfred Evans is renowned for his prize-winning in Wales and beyond. This kindly, gentle, diffident, elderly Welshman has been the subject of both radio and television programmes; his forbears would be proud.

The Fron 🐝

The Fron, once a hive of industry on the Montgomery Canal, is now a quiet hamlet between Welshpool and Newtown. Indeed, the bus stop on the A483 is called Halfway Fron.

Where once was heard the ringing hammer of the smithy there is now the clatter of tractors and machinery from the agricultural dealer, who now occupies the site.

Traces of old lime-burning kilns can be found in gardens bordering the canal. Tan-y-Fron farm and the post office/shop have Regency metal-framed casements, each with two mullions and transom with many small intersected Gothic panes, which attract interest from architects and historians.

Over the canal bridge, No 137 – once known as Bunker's Bridge, nine houses and the mission church straggle up the steep slope of The Fron. The church, built in 1873, was once also a school. This, however, was closed in the 1920s and the children now attend Berriew primary and Welshpool high schools. The other place of worship is Providence Wesleyan chapel, built in 1839. Both church and chapel have regular Sunday services and congregations always support each other's special celebrations, such as harvest festival and anniversary concert.

Two black and white houses, two modern bungalows, and a larger modern house stand alongside the canal. Further on is Red House, an L-plan close-studded farmhouse built round a central chimney in the 17th century. Pennant, built in 1755 of red brick, has a brick dovecote and outbuildings. Further houses and council farm holdings are scattered along the main road.

It is reputed that one or two of the cottages at the top of The Fron are thought to have been tai unnos, dwellings built in the course of one night.

Four Crosses

The Montgomeryshire border village of Four Crosses is situated between Oswestry and Welshpool. In the Middle Ages the whole area now called Four Crosses was known as the village of Llandysilio and there has always been confusion over the names. The church and school are recognised as Llandysilio, but the post office, garage and village hall retain the name Four Crosses.

Some say that Four Crosses is so named because of the Roman roads which crossed in the village. According to legend, however, it is said that 'When the parish saint died there happened to be an eclipse of the sun. This eclipse caused a phenomenon which gave rise to four equally spaced shadows of the tower cross to be cast down on the four sides of the church.' (*History of Llandysilio*).

The present church of St Tysilio replaced an earlier one which was demolished in 1867. In the churchyard there are yew trees which, according to church documents, are well over 250 years old. The original schoolhouse was sited near the church, but in 1896 a new church school was built. Today it is not used because of structural defects and the children are taught in mobile classrooms.

After a few years of hard work and fund raising by the villagers a new community centre was built behind the school. Known as the Village Centre, it is used by the various organisations in Four Crosses and neighbouring areas.

Nowadays there is no village 'bobby', so the police station is a private dwelling. The railway station, too, is a thing of the past – Beeching's axe fell! Where the station was, the Milk Marketing Board now provides work for over 100 men and women at the Creamery, which is famous for cheese-making, 4,000 tons being made each year from milk supplied by 158 local farms.

No longer does the village blacksmith tend his forge. A small engineering firm has established itself where once one could watch the sparks fly as the horses were shod. Horses once played a most important part in the farming community. Local farmers travelling to the neighbouring markets would ride their horses to Four Crosses and stable them at Four

Crosses Inn or the Golden Lion and then journey by train to Oswestry or Welshpool. There was a Smithfield behind Four Crosses Inn and during the First World War cattle were brought there to be graded. Today it is used as a car park.

Many of the farmhouses and other dwellings in the parish date back to the 1700s, but only a few remains of the old Rhysnant Hall, home of the Penrhyn family, can be seen.

It is around here that the legend of Little Jack Red Cap is woven. There are varying stories concerning the son and heir of the hall, but some say that he was attacked and killed on his way home from school. His parents were naturally heart-broken and for years afterwards Jack's ghost haunted his home. Unfortunately, this upset the servants and they refused to stay. It was decided that the ghost must be captured and after many nights of trying to catch him, the ghost changed into a moth, was caught and placed in a bottle. The bottle was thrown into a well and even now, when there are strong winds blowing, Little Jack Red Cap is supposed to return to haunt the grounds.

Running through the village is Offa's Dyke, built eleven centuries ago by the Mercian King Offa to separate the Welsh from the Mercians. It is a common occurrence to see hikers 'walking the dyke'.

The river Vyrnwy winds its way along the edge of the parish and gives pleasure and sport to anglers. The canal, which was once used for traffic, is now overgrown with reeds but provides a haven for wildlife.

Guilsfield

Guilsfield is in a pleasant sheltered valley, about three miles north of Welshpool, in which flow two brooks. On the south side is the Rhyd y Moch, and the village itself is on the Bele brook. The two join at Varchoel and flow on to join the river

Cottages at Guilsfield

Severn at Pool Quay. The old name of the village is Cegidfa, and signifies a place abounding in hemlock.

Guilsfield has grown more rapidly since the Second World War than any other village in the old county of Montgomeryshire. A landmark was reached in its local government history in 1987 when the residents elected their first councillors to the new Community Council. Prior to that, since 1894, it had been divided into two parts. Guilsfield Within was part of one of the wards in Welshpool Borough, and Guilsfield Without was under the jurisdiction of Llanfyllin Rural District Council. It now has a population of about 1,270.

The parish church in the village centre is dedicated to St Aelhaiarn, and is one of the finest in Powys. There has been a church on the site since before AD 600. The existing tower is 12th century, but the remainder is 14th century. It is notable for the beautiful painted ceiling over the chancel.

A wall surrounds the church and churchyard, and it is one of the few in Wales with a road all round it. There are several interesting listed houses around the church.

The churchyard is closed for burials, but there is a cemetery a short distance away. Memorials to those who died in the First and Second World Wars are to be found in the church and on a war memorial at the cemetery. West of the village is Cloddiau Cochion, home of a noted Quaker, Richard Davies, and nearby a Friends' burial ground.

Until the increased development of houses the population was mainly agricultural. It still has some first class stock and arable farms in close proximity to the village, but commuters travel daily to work in Welshpool, Newtown, Oswestry and Shrewsbury. It has a thriving Agricultural and Horticultural Society which holds a show annually.

Whilst a lot of shopping is done in the nearby towns, the village does have a grocery store and a busy post office and shop. There is a petrol station and garage in the middle of the village, and petrol pumps at a garden suppliers at Groes llwyd. The two public houses are the King's Head Inn and the Oak Inn. There is a small caravan site at Derwen, and a larger site at Hidden Valley, Maesmawr.

Gone are the butchers, cobblers, blacksmith, wheelwrights and millers. Members of the local Tanatside Hunt have to look further afield for a smith. The last surviving mill ceased working in 1940.

The area has a long history of Nonconformity dating back to the 17th century. The existing Presbyterian church was built at Groes llwyd in 1883. The chapel at Geuffordd was built in 1870, enlarged in 1880, and a schoolroom and chapel house added at a later date.

Guilsfield county primary school was completed in 1963, and has a large hall which is also used as a community centre. As well as playing areas, it has a football ground and cricket pitch. When the church school, which was built in 1832, ceased to be used, it was bought by Miss Bridget Jackson, and given to the village for community use, for which it has proved invaluable.

There are six early British settlements in the locality. The one on Gaerfawr Hill, overlooking the village, is now owned by the Woodland Trust. It is accessible along well trodden paths, and the views from the top are worth the walk. The others are Broniarth, Clawdd, Clawdd Llesg, Pantmawr and Cefn du, all on hill tops.

In a little dell near Greiddyn is an ancient holy well where it was customary for local children to make a pilgrimage on Trinity Sunday, until the Second World War. Clawdd Spout is another such well in the middle of a wood at Maesmawr.

Near Crowther's Coppice, the famous Guilsfield hoard of bronze implements, now housed in the National Museum of Wales in Cardiff, was found.

Cobham's Garden was the scene of the capture of Sir John Oldcastle, Lord Cobham, the Lollard leader and rebel, in 1417. He is said to have been the model for Shakespeare's Falstaff. One of Guilsfield's modern estates has an avenue named after him.

A farewell party for estate tenants and employees at Garth Hall in 1946 marked the end of the long connection of the Mytton family with Garth estate. The hall and park were bought by Montgomeryshire County Council, and four smallholdings formed. The hall and round stable block were later demolished.

Other notable houses in the area are Trawscoed Hall, an 18th century house set in its own grounds, which enjoys a commanding position overlooking Groes llwyd; and Trawscoed Hen, which was partly destroyed by fire in 1858, where the local hunt kennels are housed.

Maesmawr Hall, built in the reign of William and Mary, replaced a house burnt down in the Civil War. It has a Victorian addition built by a Mrs Curling. She also built Brookland Hall in 1864, which now houses Powis College, a private school. Also of interest are Trelydan Hall, and several farmhouses.

Hyssington village green

Hyssington 🌿

Hyssington is a tiny village on the slopes of Corndon Hill, much loved by its inhabitants. A narrow road winds uphill to the village green, chapel, post office, old school and village hall, and continues steeply past the turning to the church, to the south-facing slopes of Corndon Hill.

No new houses had been built in Hyssington for over 100 years until the 1970s. Now there are new bungalows amidst the landscape of traditional grey stone dwellings. There is a mixture of old established families and newcomers from afar.

The old school closed in 1966 and since then local children have attended Churchstoke primary school. The schoolhouse has been converted into a dwelling, as have The Pinfold, once an inn near to which cock-fighting took place in a natural amphitheatre, the Old Smithy and the Malthouse.

On the village green the old pump still stands, no longer in use, and hidden from view, the old horse well.

The village lies within a less favoured area for farming, the soil being shallow on boulder clay. It is predominantly a stock-rearing area. Small farms are disappearing but there are three British Friesian milking herds.

Just down the road from the village is the Llanerch Herd of Welsh Mountain Ponies, two of which were selected for use by Prince William.

Hyssington was once well known for its Girl Guide company, founded and captained by the late Miss Hethir Kay, who was Chief Commissioner for Girl Guides in Wales from 1944 to 1954.

The church, restored in the 1890s, is dedicated to St Etheldreda, a Saxon princess who became an abbess. The first record of a church on the present site is in the 13th century, but it is likely one existed here in late Saxon times. The circular churchyard was perhaps part of the motte and bailey castle which overlooks the church. On Castle Hill there is a fine, and famous, rookery.

Under the church steps, legend has it, lies the miniaturised body of the Bull of Bagbury, which tormented the villagers in the early 19th century. An irascible farmer living at Bagbury Farm was cursed by a witch. His soul took on the form of a bull, which was eventually driven into the church and exorcised by twelve priests. The bull shrank until it could fit into a small box, and was placed under the church step – which has not been moved since. Strange markings on the step are reputed to have been caused by the bull's hoofs.

The Methodist chapel, built of grey stone with white brick dressing, is in the Bishop's Castle and Clun Circuit and has a membership of 19. It dates from 1889.

Corndon is a conical hill formed by the intrusion of

dolerite into the Ordovician shale and rising to over 1600 ft above sea level. There are six round cairns on the hill with further examples on the lower slopes, probably of Bronze Age date. Although several appear to have been opened at some time, there are no records of any burials having been found. To the north of Corndon and on its lowest slopes, a stone circle, the Whetstones, stood until all traces were removed by gunpowder in 1860.

Hyssington once had an axe factory midway between the village and Corndon. Stone axes were made and sold across the country, one being found near the Wash on the east coast of England.

One mile west of Hyssington the rounded and rocky summit of Roundton Hill is encircled by an Iron Age hill fort. Its 87 acres have been bought by the Montgomery Trust for Nature Conservation. The hill has archaeological and geological interest as well as high landscape value and important wildlife.

Rare plants have developed on its volcanic soil and over 100 lichen species are recorded. The hill supports breeding pairs of kestrel, wheatear, whinchat, treepipit and redstart among other birds, and peregrine falcons can be seen in the winter. There is also a colony of two bat species, the Daubenton bat and the globally rare lesser horseshoe bat.

Kerry

Kerry lies on the south-east border of Montgomeryshire, on a spur of the Kerry Hills. Across these hills runs the Ridgeway, an ancient track, where burial mounds of Bronze Age date are found. Kerry Pole marks an intersection of two mountain roads. On either side of the valley can be found earth mounds of the Norman period, the finest example being a motte and bailey close to the old vicarage.

The public water tap at Kerry

St Michael and All Angels' church is the focal point of the village. Rebuilt in 1176, its re-dedication saw an extra-ordinary confrontation between the Bishop of St Asaph and Giraldus Cambrensis of St David's, each claiming the church and parish for his diocese. They excommunicated each other, but victory eventually went to Giraldus, the bishop departing pursued by sticks and stones thrown by the local people. The church was transferred amicably to St Asaph in 1849.

By ancient custom, part of the sexton's duty used to be to perambulate the church during services and, finding anyone dozing, to ring the 'Little Ting Tang Bell'. Fear of such kept everyone alert!

There is a Welsh Bible, printed in Oxford in 1690, chained to the lectern.

Outside the churchyard gates is The Square, once the venue of open air gatherings, now a car park.

Of four inns in the village listed in the 1835 Tradesmen's Gazette, only The Herbert Arms, known as 'The Top', and The Kerry Lamb, known as 'The Bottom', remain. The east of the square was once familiarly known as 'Up Street' and the west as 'Down Street'. Kerry had its blacksmith, wheelwright, shoemaker and tailor. Now there are two shops, a post office, fish and chip shop and garage. Builders, painters, hauliers and a double glazing company are based in the village, but mostly workers commute to Newtown. Although it is a farming community, few people these days find work on the land, but, happily, there is little unemployment.

Formerly, each cottage had its own pigsty and garden, or a patch on the allotments laid on glebe land for 'the labourers of Kerry'. Still to be seen are remains of the old public water tap, inscribed 'Waste Not Want Not 1849'.

In the village street stand two attractive dwellings, built in Gothic style in 1818, which were the lodges which once commanded the entrance to Dolforgan Hall. The village and farms around were once divided between the estates of Dolforgan and Brynllwarch.

Early in the 19th century the latter was the home of William Pugh, JP, who played an important part in bringing both canal and road to Newtown, and thus the flannel industry with consequent prosperity. Pugh himself lost a fortune and died in Caen in 1842.

His estate was bought by John Naylor, a good landlord who renovated his properties so that few old buildings remained. Houses east of the square were among those restored, or rebuilt in red brick, and the thatched cottages disappeared. In 1951 Brynllwarch Hall was opened by Montgomery District Council as a residential school for boys.

The Baptist chapel was built in 1824, the most recent

improvements being carried out by members of its congregation in 1982.

In 1968 the school's centenary celebrations included an old scholars reunion. Improvements were carried out in 1987, a new wing being added, and recently a conservation area was created in a corner of the school field, 85 pupils each planting a tree. The first recorded school dates back to 1714 and in 1788 a Sunday school was established, possibly the first in Wales.

The village has given its name to one of the finest breeds of sheep in Britain – the Kerry Hill. The breed is covered, except for face and legs, with a fleece of white wool and, being hardy, will adapt to all climates. In 1988 it won the Supreme Inter-Breed Championship at the Royal Welsh Show.

Each year on 16th September was the annual Kerry Fair, when hurdles were pushed onto the cobbled pavements and sheep pens filled both square and street. There were no auctioneers, farmers haggled between themselves. The railway came in 1863 and hundreds of sheep would be transported to the main line at Abermule. The fair left the street in around 1916 and organised sales were held in a field behind the school. Today one sale is held in September at Glanmeheli, a nearby farm. The station closed to passengers in 1931 and was finally axed in 1956.

In 1888 John Naylor constructed a tramway, an extension of the railway, to connect with his sawmills. It ceased to run in 1895 but was used again in 1917 in connection with the prisoner of war camp at Blackhall. Naylor's sawmill is now part of a conservation area and nearby is an exhibition gallery.

Kerry villagers are keen gardeners and the annual show is of a high standard. Children have their own competition and there is a Best Kept Garden contest, with gardens open on a Sunday in September.

The bowling green's opening in 1982 was a proud event

for the dedicated men who had laid the green by voluntary labour. It is so good that county games are played there.

Still held in June, the village Eisteddfod maintains the tradition handed down from the Rev John Jenkins (Ifor Ceri), vicar of Kerry, who first fostered the idea of the National Eisteddfod in the early 1800s.

New housing estates have grown up and village organisations have multiplied. The village hall, built in 1957, replaced the reading room, so called because penny readings were held there after it was erected by Naylor in 1856.

Footpaths afford lovely walks around the district, and for both locals and new arrivals it is a delightful place to live.

(Thank you to Mr H. Noel Jerman, C.B.E., M.A., F.S.A., for permission to quote from his book *Kerry, the Church and the Village*.)

Leighton 🌿

Leighton is scattered over the western slopes of Long Mountain, extending from the Severn valley to the Beacon Ring, 1,000 ft above.

Much of the village was built in the 1850s when John Naylor was given an estate at Leighton as a wedding present. He demolished the old hall and built a fine new Gothic-style hall and a model estate, with exotic animals in the park and every modern convenience for the hall and farm. His funicular railway and private gas supply have ceased to function, but many of his works are still in use. The church, for instance, completed in 1853, is a miniature cathedral, with a fine spire and flying buttresses.

The Naylor family sold up the estate in 1931 and at present the hall is empty. The massive block of home farm buildings now houses not only six farms, but also seven light industries which occupy the huge round piggeries and mill buildings. Leighton Woods continue as commercial and sporting woodlands but with thriving widlife, including buzzards, badgers and polecats. The redwood trees, brought in pots from California for Naylor's pinetum, are now a grove of massive trees probably unique in Britain. A Grand Fir here is thought to be the tallest tree in Britain.

Leighton has no pub or shop. It has a post office in a garden shed, and a village newsletter which has become essential reading. The Victorian primary school has 34 pupils and the modern village hall adjoining it has given rise to a thriving playgroup and various sports clubs. The need for money to replace the old guild room united the village in a frenzy of fund raising, and the duck race on the river, which was part of this, has become an annual event!

Offa's Dyke runs through Leighton, and the road along the top of the mountain was an old drovers' road. Nowadays, the main road becomes the Dragon Route for holidaymakers in summer, and every Monday is busy with a never-ending stream of Land Rovers and trailers taking sheep and cattle to Welshpool market two miles away. Possibly it will be quieter when the proposed Welshpool bypass is built across the valley.

The most obvious occupation is dairying and stock rearing, but other businesses in the village include agricultural and motor engineers, builders, kitchen furniture makers, road surfacing contractors, haulier, boarding kennels and photo-litho artists for the printing trade.

'Leighton Bottom' is known to birdwatchers as the haunt of rare wildfowl in winter. Several families in the village specialise in keeping rare breeds of farm animals and domestic fowl, and llamas can often be seen near the church!

On the top of the mountain is the village of Trelystan, a scattering of farms sheltering in the folds of the hill, and extending as far as the English border. Trelystan is famous for its tiny, half-timbered church across the fields, which, like Leighton church, is a Welsh parish in the diocese of Hereford. There are indications of a Dark Age churchyard on the site of the present yew-dark graveyard.

Two round barrows on the top of the mountain have been excavated and signs of an earlier Beaker settlement of around 2000 BC have been found underneath. Beacon Ring is an Iron Age fort dating from around 500 BC, somewhat spoilt by the trees inside it, planted to commemorate the Queen's coronation in 1953. The two television masts beside it are the modern version of the beacons of times past.

Llanbrynmair 🌿

Three stone circles on the top of Newydd Fynyddog are evidence of early human habitation in the parish of Llanbrynmair. The present parish, eleven miles in length and seven in breadth, is made up of one major and seven smaller settlements, lying along three valleys, those of the Twymyn, the Rhiw Saeson and the Iaen rivers.

The rivers meet near Tafolwern and all the water in Llanbrynmair drains to this spot, the lowest ground in the area. In earlier times, this made it very marshy and so, combined with the dense forest which covered much of the low ground, it was easy to defend. It is not surprising, therefore, that Tafolwern, which means 'the dock leaf meadow', was the ancient seat of Owain Cyfeiliog. The remains of the 12th century motte and bailey castle can still be seen in the shape of a mound which, in spring, is covered with daffodils.

One of the oldest, but still inhabited, houses in the district is Plas Rhiw Saeson, the Mansion of the Hill of the English. This dates from the 11th century and is situated beyond the hamlet of Pandy. It stands at the meeting of two valleys, one

Llanbrynmair village shop

leading to Mawddwy and North Wales, the other to Welsh-pool and England. Pandy lies in the north of the parish and is one of the five pandys, or one-time fulling mills, an indication of the importance of the woollen industry to this area in the 19th century.

Today the largest settlement, which includes the war memorial and the school and community centre, is clustered around the Wynnstay Arms, an old posting house on the main road from Newtown to Machynlleth, which was originally a turnpike road completed in 1821. To the south-east, along the main road, lie Dolfach (the little meadow) and Talerddig (Erddig's brow). An older turnpike road led from here, over the hills and down to a bridge over the river Twymyn at Bont Dolgadfan, and then over another pass to Machynlleth. Bont was once a thriving community of people engaged in the woollen industry, started by a small colony of Flemish weavers who settled there in the 17th century.

The parish takes its name from the church (Llan) on the hill (Bryn) of St Mary (Mair), which today dominates the hamlet of Llan. The present building dates from the 14th century but it is generally thought that a church was founded here by St Cadfan (hence Dolgadfan, the meadow of Cadfan) in the 7th century. However, an oft-quoted legend relates that an attempt was made to build a church in a nearby meadow and that every night what had been put up during the day was mysteriously pulled down, with the warning 'Dol gâd y fân', meaning 'Forsake the meadow', offering another explanation of the name.

At the south-western end of the parish, along the Twymyn valley, lies the hamlet of Pennant (the head of the ravine) and beyond that the spectacular waterfall, Ffrwd Fawr, where the river Twymyn, which rises just beyond at Dylife, falls a hundred feet into the Pennant valley. It is difficult to appreciate its full beauty, even on foot, because access is not easy, so it remains a quiet and unspoilt beauty spot.

Alongside the main Newtown to Machynlleth road runs the Cambrian Railway, opened in 1861, entering Llanbrynmair through what is said to be the deepest cutting in the British Isles, at Talerddig. Trains no longer stop in Llanbrynmair and it is necessary to travel eight miles by road to the nearest station.

A unique geological feature of Llanbrynmair is the 'Natural Arch', near the railway cutting. This looks like a regularly built blind arch made from large squarish stones, but it was created naturally as the land formed and settled over thousands of years.

There are records of a charity school, part of Dr Williams' foundation, in the 17th century. In the 19th century there was both a National school and a British school. The buildings are still there, now converted to homes, as is the Bont school, built in the early 20th century and closed in the 1960s.

Llanbrynmair is linked to Machynlleth not only by the modern trunk road and the older, narrow mountain road over the hills, but also by the long distance Owain Glyndwr Footpath which circles the parish to the south and west towards Machynlleth and then comes back parallel to the main road before striking off over the hills to the north.

The parish includes a large portion of mountainous land, shared amongst the farms which lie along all three valleys. These concentrate mainly on sheep farming and most are family concerns.

The flannel industry was vital to the economy of this part of Wales in the 18th and 19th centuries but, although a factory was built in Bont Dolgadfan around 1800, it was very much a cottage industry and was killed off by the large-scale operators in the north. Some men worked in the lead mining industry, either at Ty Isaf near Pennant, or further afield, at Dylife. Nowadays, apart from the people who farm, the community houses forestry workers, and people who provide services and each morning a mini-bus and cars take a wide range of workers to the Laura Ashley factories in Carno, Newtown and Machynlleth. The area has proved very attractive to craft workers and artists of various kinds; some work from home, others occupy the complex of craft workshops near the Wynnstay Arms. High quality products created in Llanbrynmair are sold all over the world.

There is a strong tradition of nonconformity. The Independents or Congregationalists held services for over 60 years in a lean-to at Tymawr Farmhouse until Hen Capel (Old Chapel) was built at Dolfach in 1739. In 1767 the first chapel of the Calvinistic Methodists was built in Bont. At one time there were ten or eleven chapels around the area; nowadays only two are used regularly. Others were converted into homes or are used occasionally for special services.

The nonconformist chapels were the places where radical

views were expressed and developed in the late 18th and 19th centuries and Llanbrynmair was a centre of radical ideas and thought. This unrest, combined with the decline of the woollen industry in the area, led many people to emigrate to America during this period. The son of two early emigrants, William Bebb, became Governor of the State of Ohio in 1846. Nowadays there is a steady stream of Americans and Canadians who come in search of their roots, while many of the long-standing inhabitants have relations in the USA and Canada.

At the centre of local radicalism was Samuel Roberts, known as S.R., who was born in 1800 at the Hen Capel house. As well as being a writer and preacher, he worked on the farm at Diosg, and he was ordained in 1827. He campaigned for a multitude of causes, including agricultural reform, the abolition of slavery, a railway in his area and a cheaper postal service and, as well as writing regularly for newspapers and magazines, he edited his own monthly periodical, *Y Cronicl*.

It is known that travelling poets used to visit the old house at Rhiw Saeson and there is a strong poetic tradition in Llanbrynmair. One of the most famous poets was Richard Davies, born in 1833. He farmed with his parents at Fron but devoted his leisure to mental improvement and to music and poetry. He wrote, amongst other things, *Sospan Fach* and *Llanbrynmair i mi*, and took the bardic name of Mynyddog from Newydd Fynyddog.

A more recent 'famous son' is Iorwerth C. Peate, born 1901. He grew up in what was then a monoglot Welsh-speaking community, went to university and developed a great interest in history and archaeology. He became a scholar and poet and went on to be the first curator of the famous Welsh Folk Museum at St Fagan's, Cardiff.

The most picturesque customs still practised locally are connected with the wedding ceremony. A bridegroom and his friends were barred from the bride's house immediately before the wedding and today tractors and araldite have been used to block the bride's path to chapel or church! When the wedding party returned from the ceremony, children halted their progress by throwing a rope across the road and keeping it there until they were given coins. Today, the ropes are decorated with ribbons and flowers and bridegrooms come well prepared with small change.

Such a rural area, some 14 miles from the nearest town, is lucky to have one unusual facility – a privately run sports centre, providing somewhere to swim and play squash. Barlings Barn was created a few years ago and attracts visitors to the area, as do the opportunities for walking, pony trecking and cycling.

Llanbrynmair is in the Welsh-speaking part of Montgomeryshire and for many, Welsh is their first language, but it is an area with many attractions for incomers and the local Welsh language classes are well attended by those who wish to feel really at home in this charming and beautiful community.

Llandinam ❧

Llandinam, population 350, is the most beautiful small village in Britain – and that's no fairy tale! It lies between the hills of the Severn valley, on the busy A470 road to South Wales.

Villagers travelled to London in December 1988 to receive the Beautiful Britain in Bloom award for a village with under 500 inhabitants. Before the Beeching 'axe' closed the railway in 1962 the village stationmaster, Mr Trow, regularly took first prize for floral displays on the Central Wales line. The village continued to win prizes for neatness and floral displays, being Best Kept Village in Wales on two occasions, winning its section in Wales in Bloom in 1988 – which led to the supreme accolade. In 1986, the villagers boast, the Queen made an unscheduled stop in Llandinam during her visit to the area.

The prefix Llan in the village name signifies church, and Dinam, or, more correctly, Dinan, a fort and the valley has been the scene of many a conflict. On the western side are the remains of a Roman encampment commanding an extensive view of the countryside and it is said to be here that Caradoc fought the Roman General Ostorius in the year AD 51.

The houses are mainly timber-framed, mellow brick and grey stone. The oldest dates back to 1692 and, until 1938, had a thatched roof. People not engaged in agriculture are employed in the neighbouring towns Llanidloes and Newtown.

Sadly, over the years, some of the well-known landmarks have disappeared, including the communal bakehouse given to the village by Captain Crewe-Read, where families such as those of Manuel, Davies, Waite and others each had an allotted day for baking.

Two notable men were born in Llandinam during the 19th century. David Davies rose from humble origins to become the owner of Ocean Collieries in the Rhondda valley and, according to the 1881 census, employed 3,000 men. He was also responsible for building Barry Docks and the Cambrian Railway in mid-Wales and became MP for Cardiganshire. A statue to his memory stands in the village centre. When it was unveiled over 1,000 people were present and were entertained to lunch by his son Edward.

On a hill overlooking the village is Broneirion, a house built by David Davies so that he could see the bridge and railway which he built and the chapel where he worshipped. The house is now the Welsh Girl Guide Training Centre, where Princess Margaret lunched when the association celebrated its Diamond Jubilee in 1970. The Davies family still live in the village, at Plas Dinam.

David Kinsey was the other famous son of Llandinam. In his time he was village postmaster, parish clerk, schoolmaster, reporter, poet, diarist and monumental sculptor. Evidence of the latter can be seen in the village churchyard and his diary, now in the National Library of Wales, Aberystwyth, contains a wealth of information about Llandinam in the mid 19th century.

A custom in the district was the New Year's Gifting, when children visited houses singing:

'We wish you a Merry Christmas and a Happy New Year,
A pocketful of money and no more beer.
A right good fat pig to last you all the year,
Please to give me a New Year's gift.'

Llandinam, in 1904, was one of the first rural parishes in Wales to have electricity. The charge was one shilling per light per year. No wonder some people left their lights on all night!

Gordonstoun school was evacuated to the village during the Second World War and former pupils remember the happy times spent here.

Llandinam today has a Presbyterian church built in early French Gothic style, the greater part of the cost having been borne by David Davies, the contractor. It was opened in 1873 and has a remarkably fine three manual organ.

The church of St Llonios has a history going back to AD 520 and the present church was restored in 1864–5 by G. E. Street, RA, the eminent Victorian architect. The old font is deeply scored with incisions, said to have been made by Oliver Cromwell's soldiers.

The flourishing primary school was built on its present site in 1884 and its numbers have more than doubled over the last few years.

In 1868 the present inn, The Lion, had its name changed from The Mermaid when its rival, The Red Lion, closed.

At one time the village had two grocer's shops, a post office, butcher, blacksmith, haberdasher and stationer. Today there is a post office combined with a general store, where one may buy almost anything from sweets to a smoke detector. There are also weekly visits from a mobile butcher, baker, greengrocer and fishmonger.

In the centre of the village is the village hall erected by Edward Woolley, a local builder, in about 1910. It is probably one of the finest in the county with its oak panelled rooms, and is a meeting place for various organisations. These include, of course, the Women's Institute whose members completed a wonderful tapestry of 22 houses and buildings in the village in time for the institute's 70th birthday celebration in October 1988.

Llandrinio 🌿

Many years ago the Cymerau Inn, Llandrinio stood at the confluence of the rivers Severn and Vyrnwy. At a time of flood the family from the inn attempted to cross the Severn, hoping to reach safety at Crew Green. Sadly, the boat overturned and all were drowned. Their home was never lived in again after the tragedy and has now disappeared. All that remains to be seen are three pine trees, indicating that the inn had been a stopping place for drovers. The trees could be seen from a great distance and were planted as a sign to drovers that accommodation could be had there both for them and their animals. In England yew trees were planted to convey the same message and in many places the trees remain long after the buildings are no more.

Prior to the erection of the argae, or embankment, in 1790 a major part of the village was subject to flooding.

The Cymerau had a cockpit beside it and boatmen – coracles were much used there for fishing – would bring their

View of the three pines marking the site of the Cymerau Inn, Llandrinio

cockerels to do battle and would bet on their favourite. The district, Haimwood, was also well-known for its abundance of damson trees.

Llandrinio parish lies between the two rivers on the English–Welsh border and enjoys fine views of the Breidden, the Berwyns and of the cliffs at Llanymynech. The Severn runs along the southern edge of the village and the road from Wales to the Midlands crosses the river by a hump-backed bridge. Built in 1775 and repaired in 1977, it was the first stone bridge to be built on the Severn between its source and Shrewsbury.

Offa's Dyke, at the western end of the village, attracts many walkers.

There has been a church at Llandrinio since the 6th century. When it was first built it was dedicated to St Trinio, but in the 14th century King Edward II granted a concession to the village allowing a three day fair annually on the festivals of St Peter and St Paul. So on the 28th, 29th and 30th June, people came from far away to buy and sell their wares and from that time the church became known as St Trinio, St Peter and St Paul.

The bell commemorates the restoration of Charles II and bears the loyal inscription '1661 Rergcns God Save The

King'. The Holy Communion plate dates back to 1680 and the registers to 1662. The beautiful tapestry kneelers have been worked by parishioners in recent years.

Structurally, of course, the church has seen many changes over the centuries, and the rectory underwent an important change of use when it became a residential home for the elderly.

The Methodist chapel is situated at Rhos Common and is a centre for much activity. It was built in 1907 and a hall added in 1959.

Children attend junior schools in Four Crosses and Arddleen and then go on to Welshpool high school. The old village school, which closed in 1970, is now used as an Outward Bound Centre by Wolverhampton Education Authority.

Llandrinio has had a village hall since 1921, when a piece of land was made available by the Bryn-y-Pys estate and a sectional ex-Army building was purchased and erected. Over the years this was extended and repaired until, finally, in 1985, a decision was made to build a completely new structure and improve the facilities.

HRH Prince Charles visited the village in 1981 and planted an oak tree in the playing field to commemorate the occasion. There the annual fete is held and a new Rose Queen crowned every year.

Llandyssil

Llandyssil is a small village and many people do not know of it, because one does not have to pass through it to reach another destination. However, it is very accessible – seven miles from Newtown, ten from Welshpool and three from Montgomery.

The foundation stone of the present village church was

laid in 1863. The old church, which was situated on a rise overlooking the village, was pulled down in 1865 but the porch was left standing. There has not been a resident vicar since about 1976, since when the church has been grouped with Tregynon and later with Montgomery.

Panelling from the pews in the old church was used in the building of the school, which was probably erected at about the same time as the new church. The school, which closed in 1951, used to be at the foot of the hill on which the old church stood.

There was a Methodist chapel, which held services until 1983. It was built in 1863 and was included in the Newtown circuit for preachers.

The village has a wheelwright, undertaker, carpenter and builder, although the need for wheelwrighting has gone with increasing mechanisation. Until 1940 there was a blacksmith in the village and from the end of the 1930s until approximately 1957, a maltster. He used to supply the farmers with ground wheat to enable them to brew their own beer, for harvesting, threshing and sheep shearing times.

The present thriving bakery was built in 1938 and supplies bread to local people, to the nearest towns and to several villages. Before the present bakery was built the bread was baked on the premises of the village shop.

Years ago two postmen had to walk to Montgomery to collect the letters, which were then sorted in Llandyssil. Today's post office is also the village shop, which helps to make the presence of a village shop a viable proposition. Much trade is taken now by the supermarkets, because people are more mobile, having their own motor transport. Formerly, it was pony and trap to market, or 'Shanks' pony' to the village shop.

Bus services are at a premium – to Newtown and back on a Tuesday, market day, and a similar service on Saturday.

Electricity came to the village in the early 1950s; water

was brought in 1973. Before that, the only water was from the village pump or from the well known as the Common Well. Only two properties had their own wells. Washing day was really washing *all* day – and carrying all that water!

Quoits, that traditional game, was first played in Llandyssil in 1923 and many times the local team have been area champions and produced some individual champions. One old gentleman tells how the first quoiting beds were made in the orchard of the pub and the ground was levelled by hand, using spade and wheelbarrow.

Winter time is no problem in Llandyssil as there is everything to hand. Burst pipes can be repaired, there's food to eat and beer to drink, girls come to do one's hair – which helps to boost morale, and an undertaker can see to one's needs if the occasion arises! One thing is missing in the village, however. There is no resident schoolmaster, vicar or minister, someone to go to if in need of help.

Several bungalows and 20 council houses were built in 1950–51 and more new buildings are going up.

Llanfair Caereinion ✺

Since the mid 1980s Llanfair Caereinion has seen the opening of an antique-restoring business, a spinning and weaving shop, a candlemaker's, a stained-glass window enterprise, the 25th anniversary of the reopening of the Welshpool and Llanfair Light Railway, the completion of new bungalows for the elderly, and the opening of a purpose-built health centre.

Today 'Llanfair', as it is affectionately known, is a community of about 1,000 people. There used to be a direction sign pointing over the bridge leading off the Welshpool–Dolgellau road reading simply 'The Town'. Although it never received its official charter as a town, it has given important service to the surrounding countryside. It developed during the 18th and 19th centuries and declined during the 20th.

During those earlier years the town was almost self-supporting, with a thriving flannel industry and a tannery. Everything was made in Llanfair – clothes, hats, boots, farm implements such as carts and wagons, and furniture and household goods. There was a shop in almost every home in the main streets. Market day was Saturday.

Operating in Llanfair in the latter years of the 18th century was Samuel Roberts, a highly skilled clockmaker. Many fine examples of his work in grandfather clocks can still be seen in the locality and further afield. A superb example can be heard as well as seen in the Welsh Folk Museum, St Fagan's, Cardiff. There is a sundial made by him in Llanfair churchyard.

The unofficial town hall and many of the surrounding shops, inns and houses – mostly with thatched roofs – were burned in a great fire in 1758. The story made the *London Gazette* – three weeks later! Inventories made of the 'property and effects destroyed' in order to claim compensation show it to have been a prosperous little town with a well-equipped ironmongery business. A grocer even stocked coffee. One man claimed for 'the beer which had to be drunk at the time'. Presumably, this resourceful innkeeper could see the fire coming, but could not remove his beer to a place of safety!

A printing press was established in the rebuilt town hall during the 1820s. One of those who bought a Welsh Encyclopaedia by Owen Williams of Waunfawr was Prince Louis Napoleon, a nephew of Napoleon Bonaparte. He was a great scholar of Celtic languages.

Among those attracted to work there in 1840 was young John Edwards from Cefn Mawr, near Wrexham. He was born in 1813 and was a nephew of Twm o'r Nant, famous

writer of Welsh interludes. Under his bardic name of Meiri-
adog, John became a major figure in Welsh literary and
Eisteddfod circles. At the end of the century he was able to
describe himself as Wales' oldest bard. Epitaphs composed
by him can be seen in the old cemetery in Watergate Street
and in other cemeteries in the area. He spent the latter part of
his life as proprietor of the Swan Inn, which ceased to be a
public house in the early 1900s.

Three years before John's arrival in the town another
publican, John Hassal of the Red Lion, performed the difficult task of holding back a riotous crowd which was threat-
ening the life of the highly unpopular Poor Law Relieving
Officer. The officer had arrived at Llanfair to enforce the new
law which forbade the receipt of Poor Law money by able-
bodied paupers. For the young unemployed this meant either
a destination of the local workhouse in Llanfyllin or seeking
work in another town.

Today, care of the sick, elderly and unemployed is much
improved! The Caereinion Health Centre serves the surrounding district. A description of Llanfair as it is today,
written by schoolchildren and others representing a cross-
section of the community, has been placed in a box in the
foundations of this new building. The box will be opened
after 100 years.

The high school and the primary school are bilingual.
Most subjects are available through the medium of Welsh.
Because of this the catchment area for the high school
extends as far as Newtown and Welshpool. There are also
thriving mother and toddler groups conducted in Welsh and
there is a popular course for Welsh learners.

Llanfair is located in the deep Banw river valley. On odd
occasions the streams flowing from the high ground into the
Banw become raging torrents and bring havoc to home and
work places below. During the massive storm of 1958 the
gable end of a house collapsed into the river. Now it is hoped

94

that the tunnel under the town and church has averted similar dangers for all time.

The industrial estate near the light railway station provides some employment, but much of the working population travels to other towns daily. There is a livestock market every Tuesday and sheep sales on Saturdays in September.

The local council is anxious to develop the attractions of Llanfair and has initiated the construction of a footpath along the riverside as far as Deri Woods and its picnic site. Many holidaymakers visit the area, attracted by the charm and beauty around, and many of them stay at the local caravan sites. The narrow gauge railway is a special attraction.

Llanfair has a number of retail and commercial enterprises as well as those already mentioned. There are two banks, a post office, a newsagent, four grocers, a butcher, an agricultural merchant and ironmonger, an agricultural co-operative and warehouse, two cafes, two garages and, of course, the Institute for meetings. There are three places of worship, but only one resident clergyman.

Llanfechain 🐚

Llanfechain means 'church in the valley of the Cain'. It has always been considered an attractive village, mainly because of its beautiful old stone church, centred in a circular churchyard with the village road and houses curved around it and, at the lower end of the village, the river Cain flowing under a stone bridge.

St Garmon's church is early Norman. It has a half-timbered roof and stone walls. The carved oak pulpit was made in 1636 and the parish register dates back to 1597. On the church wall outside the doorway are marks said to have been made by the men of the village sharpening their arrows

Saint Garmon's church, Llanfechain

for archery practice in the churchyard. There is also an old cockpit.

St Garmon's well is some distance from the church on Ty Coch land. Water was carried from it for christenings. A yew tree said to have been planted near it by St Germanus was burnt down at the beginning of the 20th century and wood from it made into a prayer desk and placed in the church.

There are also two chapels in Llanfechain, the Wesleyan

chapel, Peniel, and the Calvinistic Methodist chapel, Soar.

There has been a settlement at Llanfechain for centuries. Roman coins have been found in a river-crossing near the bridge. Domen Castell, just off the main road and facing the river, is a fine example of a motte and bailey stronghold. It was possibly the fortress of Owain Fychan, one of the early lords of Mechain, who died in 1187.

Among the timbered black and white buildings in the village are Ty Coch, once owned by the Jesuits and used as a resting place for travellers, and the Plas yn Dinas Inn, once used as a courthouse.

At the top of the village is a stone building dating from 1832, which was once the village school and is now the village stores and petrol station.

Built in 1951, the present village school is a pleasant building surrounded by a wide area of lawns, flowerbeds and ornamental trees. It has many times won the Wales in Bloom award for the Best Kept School Gardens.

The village hall, built in 1971, is used regularly for village activities. Held annually on August Bank Holiday Monday, the village show is a popular event. There are over 800 horticultural, cookery and craft exhibits, a dog show and sports and sideshows for the children. The exhibits are shown not only in the village hall but also in the village school.

In May of each year, a two day Horse Trial Event takes place on the Bodynfoel estate and competitors come from all parts of the country.

The railway line, opened in 1863 as part of the Cambrian Railway and which linked Llanfechain with Llanfyllin and Oswestry, was closed by Dr Beeching in 1965. The village is fortunate, however, to have a daily bus service to Oswestry and Llanfyllin.

The village has a group of houses and bungalows for the elderly which was built by the council and is named Maes

Mechain. It also has a new private development of nine houses and bungalows known as the Mount which is situated near Domen Castell.

The people of Llanfechain are not just those who live in the confines of the village itself. Those dwelling on the farms and smallholdings and in houses surrounding the village associate themselves entirely with the village community and take part in all its activities.

Llanfihangel yng Ngwynfa 🌿

This small village is really a hamlet, situated half a mile off the main Llanfyllin–Llanwddyn road. It is a steep village, dominated by St Michael's church, known as the 'Church on the Hill', a landmark for miles around.

Alas, the church can no longer be used, as it is unsafe. It is known to have existed in the 13th century and until it was rebuilt in 1862 was patronised by the famous Welsh family and supporters of Owain Glyndwr, the Vaughans of Llwydiarth Hall. Their great family pew dominates the chancel. The family married into the Watkin Williams Wynn family, who then became landlords of the Llwydiarth estate until its disposal in 1946, when most of the tenants became owner-occupiers.

Ann Griffiths, 1776–1805, famous Welsh hymn writer, is buried in the churchyard. Her well-known hymns are loved and sung throughout Wales and coach loads of pilgrims visit her grave and home at Dolwar Fach, a few miles away.

On the outskirts of the village is the cemetery, a council estate of six houses, and a couple of privately owned bungalows. There is The Goat Inn at the centre, a post office/shop and the village hall, opened in 1981 and now the 'hub' of the village. Older villagers are predominantly Welsh speaking, whilst the children are increasingly bilingual. Farming is the chief occupation, mostly sheep and cattle rearing with some dairying.

Before the turn of the century Llanfihangel had a resident clockmaker—carpenter, a dressmaker, a cobbler and a visiting knife-grinder. The clockmaker ran a kind of savings club, into which thrifty folk could pay one shilling a year, so that when they married, or set up home, they could buy from him a clock, dresser, or table, depending on how much they had saved.

Today all this has gone, but one age-old custom remains, the Plygain Fawr held annually on the second Sunday in January. Parties of singers from the surrounding parishes lend their support, then after the service, all are invited for supper and the singing has been known to go on until the early hours of the morning.

The war memorial stands at the centre of the village, and behind it is a typical Welsh bwythyn (cottage), called Poplar Cottage. This was once the home of E. D. O'Brien, the gifted Eisteddfod conductor and concert compere (1911–1953). Pat, as he was affectionately called, endeared himself to all with his wit and charm. His untimely death was a great loss to Welsh culture.

Other people who greatly influenced and enhanced the cultural life of the parish were Canon J. R. Roberts, MA, rector for 43 years until his death in 1942 and Mr C. E. Shimmin, headmaster for 36 years until he retired in 1937. Both were accomplished musicians and were most successful with their respective choirs and at concerts.

A fair, known as Ffair Llan, used to be held on 9th May every year, when store cattle and sheep were sold to visiting dealers. Piglets were brought by horse and cart, with a mesh strung over to prevent their escape. With the advent of stock wagons, stock could be taken to markets at Llanfyllin, Oswestry or Welshpool.

Half a mile from the village, on the B4393, is a stone-built bridge called Pont Sgaden, Herring Bridge, so called because it was first used by a wagon carrying red herrings to be delivered locally.

Llanfihangel is reputed to have had a ghost, known as Ysbryd Ffynnon Fach (Ghost of the Little Well). A local farmer, walking home one night, did see something white and frightening there. Wondering whether to turn and run, he nevertheless decided to approach very quietly, only to find the shopkeeper's white cow happily chewing the cud! Mothers, too, used the poor ghost as a means of getting youngsters home early, by telling them it would 'get them' if they were out after midnight!

Llanfihangel yng Ngwynfa possibly derives its name from the township of Cadwnfa, later known as Gwynfa (a place in the hills) The yng Ngwynfa is added to distinguish it from all the other Llanfihangels in Wales – Llanfihangel y Pennant, Llanfihangel y Creuddyn and so on.

In this friendly parish with the formidable name, folk are known either by Christian names or house names – Jones The Shop for example – and are willing to lend a helping hand wherever it is needed.

Llanfyllin 🌿

Set in the deep wooded valley of the river Cain, Llanfyllin is a small, pleasant market community of considerable architectural variety.

St Myllin, a 6th century Celtic saint, gave the settlement its name, and the parish church, which is dedicated to him, contains a chained book. In the churchyard is the railed tomb of a Frenchman, billeted in Llanfyllin as a prisoner of war during the Napoleonic Wars, who fell in love with the vicar's daughter and came back to marry her. On the walls of an upstairs room in the house opposite, there still exist the frescoes painted by other French prisoners.

Llanfyllin has a long history and a charter granted by Llewelyn ap Gruffydd ap Gwenwynwyn, lord of Mechain, in 1293 conferred on it a mayor and council. It is easily reached from Shrewsbury, Oswestry and Welshpool, and just on the outskirts, before one reaches the quite unmistakeable former workhouse, there is a pretty stone cottage at the roadside. This was the home of the infamous Dartmoor Shepherd, who spent 39 years in jail for rifling church offertory boxes.

At the top of Market Street is the manor house and The Hall, which was a strong Catholic centre in the days of the persecutions and where King Charles I stayed when he was en route for Chirk, as the guest of Sir John Price.

The famous Welsh hymn writer, Ann Griffiths was converted at Pendref Congregational chapel in 1796. This is one of the oldest Nonconformist places of worship in Wales and was established originally in 1640. It had a turbulent history and an earlier building was destroyed by a Jacobite mob.

Just outside Llanfyllin is the mansion of Bodfach, now a well-appointed hotel. One of the ancient houses 'plasau' of North Powys and home of the Kyffin family, its gardens have one of the finest displays of azaleas and rhododendrons in Wales.

In summer, Llanfyllin is also ablaze with colour from displays of flowers in hanging baskets and window boxes. Several top awards have been won in the Wales in Bloom competition over the years. There are many beautiful walks in the area. To help the visitor, a number of them, along signposted public footpaths, are described on a list available from the local Tourist Information Office. A well-known walk is to the 'lonely tree'. St Myllin's Well, named after the saint, has recently been restored, and provides a beauty spot with panoramic views over the town.

Llanfyllin is also an ideal touring centre for Mid and

North Wales and there are some spectacular car drives such as to Lake Vyrnwy, over the moors to Bala, to the great waterfall Pistyll Rhaeadr, to Pennant Melangell and over the mountain road to Dinas Mawddwy.

Llangurig 🌿

Among the hills on the upper reaches of the river Wye, nearly 1,000 ft above sea level, lies the village of Llangurig. It has a wealth of history, customs and characters, dating from the year AD 500.

In that year St Curig, a converted warrior, arrived from Aberystwyth and built a monastery, or 'clas', on the banks of the river Wye. A clas consisted of a small church, the cells of the monks, a workroom and graveyard, all enclosed within a wall. This is how Llangurig – church of Curig – got its name.

About the year 1180 Curig's clas was disbanded. Now on the site stands a beautiful, grey stone church. Over the years renovations and improvements have taken place, but parts of the present church date from the 13th century.

One local squire who did a great deal of restoration work on the church around 1880 was J. Y. W. Lloyd, KSG, locally known as Chevalier Lloyd, of Clochfaen Hall, a large country house overlooking the village. A monument erected in his honour still stands in the village.

When his descendants Sir Harry and Lady Joan Lloyd-Verney, occupied Clochfaen Hall, Sir Harry being private secretary to Queen Mary and Lady Joan her lady-in-waiting, Prince Albert, later King George VI, stayed there. He worshipped in St Curig's church on more than one occasion, and the place where he sat bears a crown to commemorate his visits. Many people have found peace within St Curig's walls –

'Come, seek a restful moment in the church's
peaceful calm,
Where the air is cool and pleasant, 'tis a
soothing, healing balm.'

Two chapels serve the village and surrounding district, a Wesleyan Methodist and a Presbyterian Methodist.

Near the church is the village green with its special link to the past – a delightful fountain which supplies clean water for all. At one time a stone cup was attached to a chain, but this has long since disappeared. The horse trough remains and, lower down, a drinking bowl for smaller animals. A quotation from the Bible is inscribed under the arch of the fountain, 'He sendeth the springs into the valleys, which run among the hills.'

In 1863 the Manchester and Milford Railway came to Llangurig but was never completed. The old track may still be seen passing Tanllwyn Farm from the direction of Llanidloes. An arched railway bridge still spans Nant Shan at the west end of the village.

No records of serious wrongdoing around Llangurig in the past can be traced, perhaps because there was an effective deterrent in the form of a whipping post, situated where the post office and stores now stand.

There are two hotels, The Black Lion and The Blue Bell, and one guest house, The Old Vicarage. The Black Lion was once a coaching inn in the days when the stagecoach ran from London to Aberystwyth via Llangurig, providing a most welcome rest and change of horses. There is no stage now, of course, but a postal mini-bus has taken its place, the first of its kind to be run in the British Isles. The Blue Bell has remained much the same as of old, with large open fire, stone-flagged floor and black oak beams in the ceilings. All three establishments enjoy a flourishing tourist trade.

A Welsh craft shop stands opposite the Black Lion, providing quality goods for the tourist trade. The Wye Garage on the village outskirts, supplies other needs of the village.

Llangurig's population has increased in recent years, and the newcomers have either built new homes or occupied the more isolated cottages. The local people are of a warm, generous nature, friendly and kind-hearted. The village is always busy with plenty of activities. The Young Farmers' Club is an energetic group who started the agricultural show, now run by the show society and a most successful annual event.

The village is surrounded by four farms, Tanllwyn, Felin Fawr, Tynddol and Brynculla. These, and others further afield, are mainly mixed farms of sheep and cattle.

Sadly, many fascinating old characters have gone. With them has disappeared the art of the fortune teller and the 'conjuror' or wise man. These people were supposed to possess strange powers which enabled them to cure illnesses in humans and animals. One such lady lived on Pencroesau, using the mineral waters of a nearby spring to cure sickness, and earning a living as well by telling fortunes.

Another such character was known far and wide as 'Old Pantybenu'. His cures consisted of strange notes placed in sealed bottles, never to be disturbed. He would consult a book at times, which seemed to be written in code. His cures must have been effective for he was engaged time and time again.

The village postman was always a popular character, his daily round taking him through the village and out to the outlying farms. In all kinds of weather he tramped over the hills, but he was eagerly awaited for the latest news. He carried many items other than mail, such as newspapers, groceries, medicines and messages from relatives or friends. He would certainly enjoy a refreshing cup of tea before he left! That era has gone, now a post office van speeds quickly on its way, with no time to linger.

Such characters as Tom Pryce of Pantdrain, local farmer, harpist and maker of hand-carved furniture; Ted Thomas of Brynculla, farmer, wood-carver and worker of sheep-dogs and Handel Lewis, cobbler, fisherman and gifted with many talents, have gone – but have left their imprint on the community.

Llangynog 🌿

For over 200 years, until the end of the 19th century, Llangynog was the largest lead mining area in Europe, with at times a population of about 2,000. It is now a quiet farming village of about 200 people, set at the head of the Tanat valley with steep mountains on three sides. On the mountains to the north of the village are the remains of an Iron Age fort.

The main road winds through the village, crossing two rivers and heading west over the Milltir pass. The village has two pubs, two chapels and the church of St Cynog, but there were once five pubs and three chapels. Nowadays there are two shops and the post office where there used to be two butchers, three grocery shops and John Hughes Clark, monumental mason. Many of the houses, which are stone with slate roofs, were built by the quarry owners.

When mining ceased, the slate and granite quarries continued to employ local men. The arrival of the railway in 1904 enabled people to go to Oswestry to market and to the theatre on Saturday nights. The village bustled with activity, the whistle from the quarry regulating people's lives.

The 'two up and two down' cottages throughout the village often housed large families and when in 1948 the circle of council houses and bungalows was built at Dolhendre, they gladly moved into the modern accommodation. The cottages which gave so much character to the village were left to become ruins. Fortunately, many have now been restored.

The Memorial Hall was built in 1938 by the local people. Everyone contributed, some lending their horse and cart, some giving stone or wood, or their time. Once built it was well used for concerts, whist drives and film shows, a WI was formed and occasionally the Armstrong company came for two weeks to do plays and show films. When not otherwise in use the hall was open six nights a week for snooker, table tennis, darts and dominoes, there was a library and baths were available. During the Second World War soldiers who manned the searchlights on the Berwyns would come down to use the baths, and the local WVS made tea for them. Evacuees from Liverpool were brought to the hall on arrival in the village.

Wood above the fireplace in the main hall came from Ty Uchaf, the home of Cadwallader Roberts, a 17th century poet who built Ty Uchaf himself. A contemporary of Welsh poet Huw Morus of Llansilin, Denbigh, Cadwallader would walk to meet Huw over the mountains.

In the library are photographs of local preachers and poets, like John Evans, bardic name Cynog Fab, who was born in the village in 1857. A staunch socialist, he also wrote hymns for the Wesleyan chapel. Also there is Robert Richards, Labour MP for Wrexham for many years, another son of Llangynog who lived most of his life in the village.

Another local man, Tom Lloyd, taught the harp. His most famous pupil was the late Nansi Richards, Telynores Maldwyn, doyenne of Welsh harpists, especially of the triple harp, the original Welsh instrument.

Electricity was once supplied to the village by Robert Jones and his son, Owen, from their generator at the old mill. It was strictly for lights only and the degree of light was determined by the flow of water. In the autumn Owen would sometimes be seen leaving a concert if the lights were flickering, to rush down to clear the leaves from the river. They also recharged wet batteries for 6d. In 1954 MANWEB arrived, staged an exhibition of equipment in the hall and the first electric cookers, irons and kettles came to the village.

Many people still remember George Phillips, who with his horse and barrel-shaped cart collected the sewage. He also had another cart from which he sold vegetables!

Peat was once an important fuel. One farmer recalls how his mother would bake bread and cakes and cook ham for a picnic and on a fine summer day the whole family would take the horse and cart up onto the Berwyns to cut peat in readiness for the winter.

There is a family atmosphere in the village, coach trips are organised for the children – who make up a quarter of the population – and for pensioners. The school closed in 1971 and has been converted into workshops.

Llangynog people enjoy singing, in choirs, in church and chapel – and in the pubs! At Christmas time Plygains are held in the churches, when people from other villages join together and members of the congregation stand up and sing individually or in groups.

Sheep-dog trials are held in September and the mountains around the village are popular with hikers, with Lake Vyrnwy and Pistyll Rhaeadr waterfall being within walking distance.

Llangynyw

Llangynyw (or Llangyniew, to give it its more English form) lies roughly between Welshpool and Llanfair Caereinion, a scattered, mainly farming community with no shop, no village centre but, nevertheless, with a strong sense of togetherness.

'The pearl is the church', says one longtime resident. That

church stands on a hill and is dedicated to St Cynyw, a little known saint or holy man, possibly an itinerant, who settled at what became Llangynyw. Its origins go back 1,400 years, during which time it has escaped unsympathetic restoration. Old oak and cobblestones give the 15th century porch special appeal, but the pearl within the pearl is the rood screen, not in quite its original state, but still a tribute to the delicate work of the wood carvers.

The list of rectors goes back to 1537 and few congregations can have loved their rectors more, judging by the memorials to them which can be seen. One is remembered by one of the church's earliest gravestones set in the east wall, others by windows, oil paintings, a Bible and, most recently, by a sundial.

Not the longest, but perhaps the most interesting incumbency was that of Thomas Richards 1826–56. He was one of a family of eight, children of another Thomas, vicar of Darowen near Machynlleth, and the five brothers all became clerics.

The family was both literary and musical and one sister, Mary, trained the Llangynyw church singers. After Thomas's death she and her sister Jane went to live with brother Richard who was vicar of Meifod, but used to walk up to Llangynyw to church because 'the singing was better'. Several of the family are buried in Llangynyw, but, strangely, no headstones mark their graves.

The white marble monument inside the church is to Canon David Evans, not a rector, but said to be Llangynyw-born. It has a tenuous link with a great man of letters. Amongst Canon Evans' papers on his death was a letter from an acquaintance which read, 'A friend of mine of the name of Samuel Johnson talks of writing a dictionary of the English language and would be much obliged to you for sending a list of those English words which are derived from the Welsh'. The dictionary was published in 1755.

Since 1956 vicars of Meifod have had Llangynyw in their charge.

Although the tiny school near the church has not been used for its original purpose since 1966, children's laughter can still be heard there, for it is the home of one of the first play-groups to be started in the area. It is also the centre for meetings of the Mothers' Union, the Community Council and for any other gatherings of the populace. Young people tend to go to Llanfair Caereinion for their clubs and so forth, the several small chapels in the area have decreasing attendances.

Prospering, however, is David Millward's school of painting which attracts students from far away. Meanwhile his wife, Jenny Nimmo, is an author of children's stories. One, *The Snow Spider*, was portrayed on television.

Busy, too, is Cyfronydd Smithy. There the present father and son are at least the fourth and fifth generations of the Thomas family working at the anvil, though today they should be more properly described as agricultural engineers.

Near the road leading to Meifod a grassy mound is all that remains of Mathrafal the one-time palace of the Princes of Powys, destroyed in 1212. Y Gardden, hill fort of 1000 BC stands guardian over all.

Llanidloes ✣

Llanidloes is centrally situated between North and South Wales, and has the distinction of being the first settlement on the Severn, the source of which is ten winding miles up in the Plynlimon hills.

King Edward I granted Llanidloes a market charter in 1280. It has wide, pleasant, tree-lined streets in the shape of a cross and in the middle is the old half-timbered Market Hall, built about 1600 and now the only one of its kind in Wales.

Beneath it is the old open market and at its north corner is the stone from which John Wesley preached on many occasions. A museum now occupies the old courtroom above, and the crib where prisoners were confined was succeeded by the Round House over the Short Bridge. This continued in use until the erection of a police station in High Street in 1864 where the courts are still held, but a new police station has been built at Glandwr.

The magnificent parish church, dedicated to St Idloes, a Celtic saint after whom the town is named, overlooks the river. The pillars of the 15th century arcade were brought from Abbey Cwm Hir, where their bases still remain. The beautiful 15th century roof with shields and angels decorating its hammer-beams, may also have come from Abbey Cwm Hir, as it was constructed at the same time. The date 1542 can be seen on one of the shields.

An interesting feature in connection with the church was the foundation of a lending library, 1688–1699, and in the 'Montgomery Collections' is to be found a 'Catalogue of books belonging to the lending library of Llanidloes church.'

There are several Nonconformist chapels in the town, all rebuilt in the 1880s when Llanidloes was at the height of its industrial prosperity. Most of them have associations with the old Market Hall, as they all held services there when their numbers became too many for meetings in private houses. The first Sunday school in Wales is said to have been held at Crowlwn in 1770.

Built in 1908, the Jacobean-style town hall was the gift of the Davies family of Llandinam. There is a mayor and corporation, and a flourishing market is held every Saturday.

A Franciscan friary was established at Penygreen in 1951 and ten years later the attractive church was built in honour of the first Catholic martyr in Wales, Richard Gwyn. A native of Llanidloes, he suffered much harsh treatment and was put to death as a traitor at Wrexham in 1584.

The old Market Hall, Llanidloes

In the 1830s Llanidloes was one of the most active centres of the Chartist reform movement and the subsequent Chartist 'rebellion'. The local weavers imprisoned three London policemen in the Trewythen Arms Hotel when they were sent by the Home Secretary to quell the unrest. For five days the town was in the hands of the rebels, but the magistrates enlisted the help of soldiers and many were captured. Thirty-two were brought before the Assizes and the leaders received heavy sentences.

The Van and Bryntail mines were a rich source of lead and were worked for many years, providing much employment for the district. In its heyday a railway was built from the Van through Cerrist to carry the lead down to Caersws. John Hughes, manager of the railway, was better known as Ceiriog, one of the finest Welsh lyric poets.

Farming has always been carried on in the district and provided the wool and leather for local factories, now sadly closed. There are several light engineering works here and the world-famous firm of Laura Ashley employs a large number of workers, mostly women, at its factory on the Station Industrial Estate.

The railway was closed in 1962 but the impressive station building, which has been restored so well in recent years, now houses small industrial units.

The population remains static, despite the building of several council and private estates. In 1953 three schools were closed and the pupils moved to a new school on the outskirts. Recently a sports centre has been opened on the school campus, and is very popular with people of all ages.

The Clywedog Dam, completed in 1967, is a great attraction for fishing, sailing and tourism. It was built to reduce flooding in the upper Severn valley and provides water for many users from Llanidloes to Bristol.

Llanllwchaiarn 🦋

The parish of Llanllwchaiarn is a joint parish of Newtown and covers an area north-east of the town, the river Severn marking the boundary between the two. The population is mainly concentrated in the area of Milford Road, Penyglodfa and Canal Road. The rest of the parish is rural, consisting of enclosed farms.

In 1815 the new Llanllwchaiarn church was built – but the vicarage lay on the opposite side of the river. This involved the vicar in either a long walk through the town of Newtown or a dangerous crossing of the river by boat. So, in 1886, a wooden bridge was built at the crossing point, known as Parson's Bridge. It was washed away during the flood of 1929.

After 1821, due to the opening of the Montgomery Canal, the village's population increased. In 1801 it was known to have a population of 675. The replacement in 1827 of an old wooden bridge which crossed the river from Newtown to Penyglodfa, enabled Canal Road and Penyglodfa to be developed as an industrial area, with many houses and flannel mills being built.

One of the district's most successful businessmen was Sir Pryce Jones, who is buried in Llanllwchaiarn. It was he who pioneered the mail order business and he also became Conservative MP for Montgomeryshire.

The village once had a school known as the Rock Grammar School for day and boarding pupils. Subjects taught included English, Latin, Greek, French, German, mathematics, natural science, music and drawing. There were two other schools in the parish, one, Penyglodfa, is in use today and was recently rebuilt. The other, Llanllwchaiarn National school, is today used as the Powys Theatre.

The canal was closed in 1937 but there are thoughts of its

being re-opened. If extended through Llanllwchaiarn to Newtown once again, it would be a boon to the surrounding district.

Llanmerewig ❧

The church at Llanmerewig, a tiny village about two miles from Abermule, has a round churchyard – no corners for the Devil to hide in, says superstition – and a connection with the Victoria and Albert Museum.

Dedicated to St Llwchaiarn, the beautiful church is the smallest in the diocese of St Asaph. It is medieval, with a bell turret at the west end of the roof, and a small south porch. The first recorded rector was the Rev Rhys, in 1500. Three hundred years later, in the incumbency of the Rev Parker, there were two restorations. Another restoration was carried out in 1892 at the expense of Mr Whitley Owen of Fronfraith, and here is the connection with the Victoria and Albert. For the consultant architect was Mr (later Sir) Aston Webb, the designer of the Victoria and Albert Museum, London.

Outside the church, on the north side, there used to be a rusty chain for fastening stray cattle, which were sold by auction after Divine Service. A vague tradition also associates it with trials for heresy. The chain has disappeared but the link remains.

The origin of the name of the parish is uncertain. The most generally accepted derivation is 'Llam-yr-Ewig', ie 'the leap of the hind', so called from the traditional folk story.

The field to the west of Cwmmule homestead, through which the path to Tyntwll passes, is called Hoar Stone. The field to the north of it is called Little Hoar Stone. A huge stone which used to stand there was taken from the hedge and used when broken up for mending roads and building walls.

At Giant's Bank there are the remains of earthworks and a camp, probably post-Roman.

Lower Maenllwyd is a half-timbered country house built circa 1580–1620. This house was for some time Llanmerewig rectory, being vacated on the building of a new rectory, and is a listed building.

Llanrhaeadr-ym-Mochnant ✍

Pistyll Rhaeadr, the famous waterfall, about four miles from Llanrhaeadr-ym-Mochnant is one of the Seven Wonders of Wales. It falls 240 ft and is a great tourist attraction.

The village itself is partly in Powys (formerly Montgomeryshire), partly in Clwyd (the old Denbighshire), 14 miles from Oswestry and 17 from Welshpool.

Most people are engaged in agriculture, the mixed farms usually run by father–son partnerships. Some of the larger farms employ local men, though fewer are needed nowadays due to mechanisation.

Everything needed for the immediate well-being of the inhabitants may be had in the village, where the shops include three grocers, a post office, a clothes shop, butcher, newsagent and hairdresser.

Agricultural supplies, household goods and other essentials can be bought at Tanat Supplies, on the outskirts of the village and within the community there are competent builders, plumbers, electricians, a furniture restorer and artists. The Sure Tex factory is the only company in mid-Wales manufacturing decorative wall and ceiling compounds. There is a haulage business and egg packing station, both employing considerable local labour. Some people, of course, find work in Oswestry and Llanfyllin. Tanat Valley Motors run an efficient bus service to Oswestry daily and holidays and day trips throughout the year.

Pistyll Rhaeadr waterfall, Llanrhaeadr

116

On the Clwyd side of the village stand the Wynnstay Hotel and the Hand Inn, the latter recently extended. On the Powys side there are the Plough and the Three Tuns. Several houses offer bed and breakfast; Y Gegin Fach and Plas-yn-Llan are licensed restaurants and there is another such at the foot of the falls four miles away.

There are three Nonconformist chapels, but only one minister, the Wesleyan minister. He is not only a good preacher but a talented artiste, called upon to entertain at parties with his conjuring tricks – a versatile man! In April 1988 a woman was appointed Deacon in Charge of St Dogfan's church and of four other churches in the area.

In 1588 William Morgan, vicar of the parish, completed his translation of the Bible into Welsh, so 1988 saw many celebrations to mark the 400th anniversary. The Archbishop of Wales preached at a service at the opening of the celebrations and the Bishop of St Asaph unveiled two commemorative plaques by the lychgate.

Once there were two schools in the village, the Green school, which was a church school built in 1858, and the Board school, which later became the Central school, where children from the surrounding area attended up to the age of 16. In 1965 the church school closed. It was sold to the Tanat Theatre Company, renovated and is now used for rehearsals and to store scenery. The company is run by two professional actors living in the area. There is a Senior and Junior Theatre Club and both present plays and musicals annually.

The public hall, opened in 1927 with a bazaar lasting two days, is the meeting place for all organisations in the village. An Eisteddfod is organised every year by the Welsh Society, the highlight being the chairing of the bard.

Historic houses in the area include Plasynglyn, an upland farm which was a port of call for monks travelling from Valle Crucis, Llangollen, to the Tanat valley. Remains of the chapel can be seen. Maesmochnant Isaf has on its land a pillar called Y Post Coch, 12 ft high and weighing six tons. Legend says it was erected to deal with a snake or dragon which might attack passing travellers. Spikes were driven into the post and covered with red cloth, against which the creature would throw itself until it bled to death! Henfache is noted as the home of the Maurice family, bitter enemies of William Morgan when he was vicar. Praying stalls used by monks can be seen in the cellar.

Llansantffraid-ym-Mechain 🦢

Llansantffraid-ym-Mechain is one of the many Llansant-ffraids established by St Bride (Sant Ffraid) who came to preach to the Welsh from Ireland, guided across the sea by oyster-catchers, which were renamed Bride's Gillies by St Columba.

Legend also has it that when the inhabitants came to build their church they chose the Foel Hill as being the highest and therefore nearest to God. One day they dragged huge stones up to the summit. The next morning all were found on the top of a rise the other side of the road. They spent the next day hauling them all back. The following morning the same thing had happened again, and again. So it was decided it must be the will of God, and the church was built where the stones were re-sited and where it now stands.

A little further up the valley Llanfechain church was also built and –

'They'd built the church and furnished it (or so the story

tells)

   And all Llanfechain waited
   The arrival of the bells.

The rutted roads were deep in mud along the valley floor,
  The wagons creaked, the horses strained,
  The draymen cursed and swore.
From Oswestry they struggled on, through mud and mire
                                          and muck,
  Across Meredydd's ford they plunged,
  At Llansantffraid they stuck.
The axles broke beneath the weight (beneath the mud
                                          as well!)
  But locals flocked to help unload,
  A crowd to every bell.
Then up the hill they toiled and strained, rejoicing as they
                                          stepped,
  They sent the carters home again,
  The bells, all four, they kept.'

Now the two parishes have been combined and the bells summon both villages to worship. There are also five chapels, but unity grows closer.

In Llansantffraid's church is a window donated by William Morris Hughes, who was Prime Minister of Australia earlier this century, in memory of his mother who died on a visit to Llansantffraid.

The parish is almost entirely surrounded by water, the Vyrnwy, the Cain, the Tanat and their smaller tributaries, which are the delineating lines of the boundary.

Fishing, not surprisingly, is popular and town clubs rent areas of the water. Until quite recently Fisherman's Sunday was held at the beginning of the season when a special service of blessing took place in church. The fishermen would clatter in in their studded waders, ready for swift departure afterwards!

Bryn Tanat, near the west boundary, was the home of a very musical family, the Leslies. Henry Leslie, who died in 1896, was a composer who had work conducted by Berlioz and whose choir twice performed for Queen Victoria. He was responsible for the origins of the Royal College of Music, and he worked with Sir Arthur Sullivan. He was also a member of the Rose Society, and the gardens of Bryn Tanat were famous for miles around.

There was once a public house adjoining the post office, until teetotallers converted the landlord, who poured away all his beer into the drains! It reopened as a temperance hotel and remained so until about the early 1900s.

Probably the most beautiful feature of the village is the bridge over the Vyrnwy. Originally it was a stone and wood structure, which was swept away by floods in 1778. The long-disused ford downstream was only usable in high summer and the fast developing trade and movement of traffic necessitated immediate rebuilding, which was completed in 1781.

There was much foot traffic in the old days. The Ffinnant Farm was a meeting place for the drovers, where they gathered with their stock to travel together to the south and to London. In many places lone oak trees were guiding marks and there is a splendid drovers' oak in one of the Trewylan fields.

The long history of farming is continued today and the flourishing Wynnstay Farmers, which started modestly in 1918, is now a huge co-operative that serves a wide area.

In 1988 archaeologists, interested by aerial photographs taken in the dry summer of 1976, unearthed evidence of a Roman supply depot, centurion's house and barracks in an enclosure of nearly three acres at the east end of the village. This depot is thought to be part of the siege camp below Llanymynech Hill, from whence the Romans attacked Caractacus (Caradog) in his last battle in AD 50.

Also because of aerial photographs in that dry summer, an ancient British settlement was unearthed on the south side of the parish at Collfryn. It consisted of wattle and daub dwellings with heavy thatched roofs, covering an area of about seven and a half acres surrounded by ditches and earthworks. The date was about 300 BC, so Llansantffraid has been a busy centre for a long time.

Two Princes of Wales have visited the village. Edward, who later became King Edward VIII, came by train and continued by car to Lake Vyrnwy. Prince Charles came by helicopter! On one occasion he inspected the work on the canal restoration, and he opened a new building at the Wynnstay Farmers on another.

The railway was closed and the lines taken up in 1965, a little over a hundred years after they were laid.

Llansantffraid is not only full of interest but surrounded by so much beauty that visitors flock into the area, staying in the two good hotels or the many bed and breakfast farmhouses and caravan sites, so the population in summer is, frequently, just about doubled.

Llanwddyn ✤

In 1988 the centenary of St Wddyn's church, Llanwddyn, ended a century of tremendous change in the area. About 100 years previously the old village, situated in the upper Vyrnwy valley, on the southern extremity of the Berwyn range, had been 'drowned' because Liverpool wanted water – and Lake Vyrnwy and the dam were constructed.

The first mention of the river Vyrnwy as a water supply was in 1865. By September 1878 trial shafts had been sunk to check for safe foundations and the proposed capacity of the dam had grown to 10,000 million gallons. It was to be the first large masonry dam – instead of an earth embankment as originally intended – in Britain. It would form the largest artificial reservoir in Europe at that time and was the first large dam to carry the overflow over its crest instead of in a by-wash channel cut into the undisturbed hillside at one end.

In July 1881 the 3rd Earl of Powis laid the first commemorative stone and in 1882 the foundation was cleared of debris and the first masonry laid. A stone quarry was opened locally and other materials brought by horse and cart from Llanfyllin. Over 1,000 men were employed and an obelisk commemorates the names of ten who were killed and 34 who died during construction.

The 'drowned' village had included a church, two chapels, three inns, ten farmsteads and 37 other dwellings. The people had to be rehoused and this Liverpool Corporation did, creating a new village downstream from the dam and building St Wddyn's church and a Calvinistic Methodist chapel.

No longer used for worship, the chapel has been made into an attractive display and information centre by the Royal Society for the Protection of Birds, the area being a reserve with a full-time warden.

About a mile below the dam the new school and community centre opened in 1950. A thriving populace now lives in modern houses using the centre's library, games room, craft room and fine hall.

An oak tree planted by King George V when, as Prince of Wales, he visited the dam, is growing strongly and a letterbox of Queen Victoria's reign – said to be one of only three remaining in the country – is set into rock near the dam crossing.

In 1890 construction started on a sporting hotel with spectacular views over the lake. Recently in new hands and refurbished, this gives employment to local inhabitants.

At some time in the 13th century, the manor of Llanwddyn came into the possession of the Knights Hospitallers of St John, who built a stone church dedicated to that saint. Other traces of the knights include the remains of a hospice on

122

Lake Vyrnwy, Llanwddyn

Mynydd Sant Ioan, near a well called Ffynnon y Myneich.

On the Dissolution of the Monasteries in the 16th century, the manor of St John, together with the tithes, passed to the Herbert family, whence they descended to the Earls of Powis, who held them until late in the 19th century.

Little is known of St Wddyn, for whom the village is named, though he is believed to be contemporary with St Melangell. He was a recluse who lived in a cell on the rock by Ceunant Pistyll, a waterfall half a mile south of the sub-merged village.

A strong Quaker community formerly existed, based on a farm called Bryn Cownwy, a room in the house being kept for meetings and an area behind the house used for burials. The last Quaker, Shon Thomas Morris, directed in his will that they be maintained. This was not observed by a later owner, but Liverpool Corporation replaced the fence round the graveyard, where 13 bodies are said to be buried.

Sardis, opened in 1822, is the only chapel in Llanwddyn, though in nearby Cownwy valley is Saron, a branch of Sardis. Montgomeryshire Preaching Festival was held at Sardis for the first time in 1961. There have been two BBC broadcasts from there and its Plygain at Christmas brings carol parties from elsewhere to join the members.

The scars left after the construction of the dam have healed and it is now a place of great beauty at all times of the day and at whatever season. The view of the lake at sunset is particularly beautiful. Sometimes, by chance, one can be there when the lake is mirror-smooth and the reflections are a perfect reverse image. After a snowfall, and looking towards the straining tower, one is reminded of castles on the Rhine.

Llanwnog 🌿

In the years prior to 1970 the village of Llanwnog, between Caersws and Carno, had remained virtually unchanged for 200 years, a close-knit, mainly agricultural community. Until 1970 only two new houses had been built there this century.

The phrase 'close-knit' has a real meaning in Llanwnog. Families have stayed and their names persist, particularly the name Wainwright.

Especially remembered is William. He pumped the church organ for 66 years, was the local baker, postmaster and shopkeeper. The post office, Vine Shop, is still in the family, kept by one grandson and his wife; another lives next door, at Vine Cottage, formerly the home of Millie Wainwright, a district nurse and the sister of William. William's sons and daughters also still live in the village.

Another family that has stayed is the Jones family of Church House Farm. John and Jean and their two sons are there now, before that was John's father, Dick, and before that his father, Zaccharias, renowned for his fine ointment. This black, waxy concoction was good for boils, whitlows and infected wounds. Horses are an important part of life at Church House, and the David Davies Hunt Pony Club members practice there throughout the year.

Harry Kinsey came of another old village family and was verger, bellringer, sexton, local choir conductor and stone-mason. He had beautiful copperplate handwriting and engraved many of the stones in the churchyard. His son, Eddie, is the present bellringer and also sometimes conducts matins.

The houses around the church, linked by a road forming a square, are of varying ages and architecture. Oldest are the black and white cottages known as Old Talbot and Gwyneira, the latter having the date 1664 over its lintel. At the north-west corner of the village, Tynllan has in its garden the remains of a tree reputed to be the one from which John Wesley preached. The house was once the home of Jessie Trow, who played the church organ for over 40 years and taught in the village school.

A new estate has been developed near the village centre on a field called Parcyrescob and more houses are planned.

Things have changed, too, in the area known as Ffynnony-corn, so called because of its proximity to the waters of a 'healing well'. The sewage scheme of 1967 cut through its source and it dried up.

The old school still stands on the south-east corner of the churchyard. It closed in 1962 after being an active church school with over 100 pupils at the beginning of the century. Later it was used for WI, Young Farmers' and Mothers' Union meetings, for concerts, dances, whist drives and as a polling station at times of local and parliamentary elections. Today, it is a rural centre for children from Dudley in the West Midlands and the village primary-age children travel to Caersws.

St Gwynog's tall, pointed spire dominates all. Its Welsh translation becomes the name of the village, which, inciden-tally, has never been Welsh in tradition or culture, but very much a border-influenced community. Established in the 6th century by St Gwynog, the church was rebuilt in the 15th century and had a major reconstruction of its west wall and bell tower in 1982, at a cost of over £25,000. Earlier in the century each Sunday there was a full quota of services, now one is held each Sunday morning, very often conducted by a lay preacher.

The vicarage stands alone to the east of the church and had its ghost, a grey figure which appeared regularly in a bed-room and on the stairs. The spirit has apparently been exorcised.

Not many village sons have served in the regular forces, but those who lost their lives in the two world wars are commemorated on a memorial in the nave of the church.

126

John Ceiriog Hughes, famous Welsh poet and sometime station-master at Caersws, is buried in the churchyard and many visit his grave.

A steep lane leads towards the hill known as the Rhallt, which is covered with fir, larch and wild cherry trees. To the left is Zion Congregational chapel which now has only one service on a Sunday and no resident minister. It is a windy spot and many a smart wedding hat has blown into a neighbouring field!

One young person said recently, 'You don't appreciate the peace of Llanwnog until you have to leave it.'

Llanwrin ✤

Llanwrin is a hamlet on the right bank of the river Dyfi, four miles from Machynlleth.

It derives its name from St Gwrin's church, which was first dedicated to Ust and Dyfrig, two saints who came over from Brittany about AD 516 under the leadership of St Padarn and his brother Cadfan. It was later dedicated to St Gwrin, grandson of Gildas, a monk-historian, born about AD 500.

The unique rood screen in the front of the church, extending across the building, is expertly carved in light oak. A large stained-glass window above the altar is very beautiful and was fitted between 1461 and 1483, in the reign of Edward IV. The rather wild facial expressions, similar to rococo style, is only found elsewhere at Old Radnor.

Besides the church there is a spacious, well-preserved rectory, now a private house where Canon Silvan Evans lived from 1876 until 1903. While rector of Llanwrin he compiled the Welsh dictionary and wrote hymns and was the first Welsh lecturer at Aberystwyth University.

Another private house was once the Presbyterian chapel, which drew congregations from a wide area, many of them walking miles to services.

In olden days the village was self-supporting. It had an inn at Tyuchaf which was also a farm, a village hall, church room, a shop and post office, butcher's shop, wheelwright, undertaker and a smithy.

Choral practice was held in the church room and there was a very successful WI which met there. The village hall is now dilapidated, but in the past it provided great entertainment concerts, Eisteddfodau, social evenings, plays and parties for special occasions. During the Second World War the Red Cross and Home Guard made good use of it, the ladies spent hours there knitting comforts for the forces and, in the summer, making jam.

The first school was a charity school held in the church room, where English was the only language spoken. In 1908 a school was opened in the village hall and in 1910 the first and last purpose-built school opened in the village. It closed in 1971.

Although a new estate of houses has been built on the old school site, the village keeps its old world charm. There is a village green and a brook, paved with cobbles, babbles its way through.

Most of the inhabitants, except a Welsh carpenter, work in the Alternative Technology Centre at Llwyngwern. They are English, but Welsh learners.

Welsh people live in the new estate and travel daily to varied occupations. In the farms bordering the village Welsh is still the first language.

It is easy to look back with nostalgia at the good old days. Better roads and everybody having their own means of transport has changed the village in some ways. Now the inhabitants can easily attend functions and meetings at the newly built hall in Glantwymyn, with its modern facilities. Villagers are able to join with a wider circle of friends and acquaintances.

Present inhabitants and their ancestors have gained immense enjoyment from Llanwrin's beautiful scenery, woodlands, farmland, lanes and footpaths. One hopes that the future generations will have the same privilege and will maintain the village way of life.

About a mile from Llanwrin is Mathafarn where Dafydd Llwyd, the poet, was squire in the late 15th century. Henry Tudor stayed with him on his way across Wales to the Battle of Bosworth, where he took the throne of England.

Llanymynech

Llanymynech, astride the Welsh–English border, six miles from Oswestry and ten from Welshpool, is neatly bisected by the busy A483 Manchester–Swansea trunk road. This partly follows the ancient boundary of Offa's Dyke. Nowadays, there is little dissension between English and Welsh. How could there be, there are two Parish Councils, two District Councils and two County Councils to see fair play!

The Aqueduct at Carreghofa, Llanymynech

Approaching the village from Welshpool, one crosses the fast-flowing river Vyrnwy by a fine stone bridge. To the right, in a commanding position, is the parish church of St Agatha, rebuilt in 1843 in neo-Norman style, no doubt to make it look much older. One of its main features is the clock, which has an extremely long pendulum. Richard Roberts, a local inventor, designed and built it. He died in 1864, the same year as the newly-built Presbyterian church opened – on the Welsh side of the street.

The main road, wide, straight and rising gently, passes through the village, over the crossroads and the canal, until it reaches the Shropshire County Stone, where it veers right. It must, for above towers the 200 ft cliff-ramparts of Llanymynech Hill, designated a site of special scientific interest to nature conservationists and industrial archaeologists alike. The 900 ft hill affords magnificent views, the village below looking like a bit of Switzerland.

In the south can be seen the flood plain of the Severn and Vyrnwy rivers. Beyond are the Breiddens with Rodney's Pillar and Criggion quarry, which has the finest green stone in the world. North and westwards lies the valley of the river Tanat and the Berwyns, stretching away towards Snowdonia. It is surprising to find a popular golf course up here. It is said that on it one can drive a ball from a tee in Wales to a green in England.

There are pre-Roman fortifications and much evidence of the Romans themselves. A local historian theorizes that it was here that Caractacus – or Caradoc – made his last stand with his faithful Britons in AD 50, before his defeat and capture, but this is a claim made for several other places in the area.

Certainly the Romans mined copper and silver here. In 1965 local boys found a cache of silver coins minted between 30 BC and AD 161 in the Giant Ogo's Cave, about which many legends abound. Other finds have included human skeletons, Roman tools, silver ornaments, pottery and battleaxes.

The years 1750 to 1910 were eventful ones for quarrying. The rocks consisted of carboniferous limestone from which lime for agriculture could be extracted. Quarries needed a substantial labour force, as did the cutting of the new Shropshire Union Canal to carry the lime away, and the building of the railway, which soon followed. It is recorded that gunpowder was first used here for underground blasting in 1692.

Around 1855 some 60,000 tons of limestone were quarried annually. The limestone was 'slid' down to the kilns, which lay alongside the new canal – one giant chimney remains. The stone was 'burnt' and the resulting lime loaded into 20-ton barges, each pulled by a single horse. It was then relayed by the national canal network to farms all over the Midlands and North Wales. The canal closed in 1946. However, plans exist for its reopening.

The railway played a big part in Llanymynech's development and around 1920 it had a busy railway junction, employing about 20 men, with 20 trains daily. The main line connected to the north through Whitchurch, Oswestry, Welshpool, Llanidloes and the coast. A branch connected with Llanfyllin, whilst a local railway, the Shropshire–Montgomeryshire, or the Potts, linked with Shrewsbury and the Midlands. The railway closed for good in 1965. Two broken piers stand in the Vyrnwy waters where the bridge once carried the beautiful green-liveried express steam locomotives and trainloads of holidaymakers to the seaside.

Two centuries of great change have encompassed Llanymynech. A hundred years ago, besides the railwaymen, bargees and quarrymen, other village craftsmen plied their trades – the blacksmith, saddler, shoemaker, tailor, linen and rope maker. There were three annual fairs and a racecourse. It was a bustling place.

Today it is no less busy. Road transport has replaced the

trains and boats. The old station has become a coalyard and a large concrete works turns out products for the building trade. There are new craftsmen in the village, mechanics, panel-beaters, paint-sprayers, TV engineers, ornamental ironworkers, bricklayers, joiners, plumbers and electricians. There is a new housing development on both sides of the border.

As leisure increases Llanymynech is prepared to meet the challenges. There are good access roads and a new bypass is planned. Services include an hotel, two public houses, fish and chip shop, three restaurants, hairdresser, petrol service station and garage, motor body repair shop and three shops, including an enterprising off-licence, post office and general stores. Three village halls provide amenities for old and young.

In the 1981 census the village population numbered 1,250. It also showed two primary schools, one each side of the border. Now only one remains, at Carreghofa for 50–60 pupils. Sadly, in 1984 the old Llanymynech school closed. For its pupils a new dawn appeared. They were to attend a splendid new primary school at Pant, one mile away. But they took with them the old school bell from Llanymynech. It now hangs by the new school entrance to summon the children promptly at 9 am each school morning.

The old school has re-emerged as a successful restaurant. School meals were never like that!

Llwydiarth

Llwydiarth, situated on the B4395 between Llangadfan and Llanfyllin, has two names – Pontllogel is the other – and is in two parishes, Llanfihangel and Llangadfan. It is believed that Llwydiarth is the older name, Pontllogel being added after the bridge was built – 'Pocket Bridge' in translation.

Saint Mary's church, Llwydiarth

The village's Llwydiarth estate came into the Watkin Williams Wynn family when long ago a Wynn married a daughter of the Vaughans of Llwydiarth, a family descended from Aleth Hen, King of Dyfed.

During the shooting season the Wynns lived at Llwydiarth Park, a house of the early 1880s. The wall surrounding the estate's 700 acres consisted of large stones, some from an ancient cairn. Under one stone workmen found a chest containing two skeletons, the head of one at the foot of the other, also an urn holding bones and ashes.

The estate had electricity in the First World War, supplied by a water-wheel, which was also used for sawing the timber in which the estate was rich. There was an estate railway for moving the timber.

In 1946 the Forestry Commission bought the estate and it became Dyfnant Forest, with employment for many. The house became the local office and flats for the workers and was sold again in 1986 to a local family.

The forest covers 6,000 acres, with 40 miles of forest roads popular for car rallies – and forest walks, and there is a picnic site by the river. Fewer men work in the forest today, contractors are brought in when necessary.

St Mary's church was built in 1883 by the then Sir Watkin, the architect being Benjamin Ferrey. Its exceptionally steep roof and commanding position make it immediately visible when approaching the village. Morning communion is held monthly, with extra services at holiday times. Years ago there were three services each Sunday and full pews. Now, the faithful few have started a restoration fund, wishing to keep the church open for future generations.

Its rose bowl and two silver vases were presented to the church in memory of his wife by a Mr Smith of Chester, one-time tenant of Sir Watkin. Mr and Mrs Smith were regular worshippers.

A tombstone in the churchyard is engraved 'Mr David Jones, 22 years agent for Sir Watkin.' Why he, among so many, was honoured by being given the 'handle' to his name is unknown!

The Presbyterian Capel Siloh, built in 1874, lies in Llangadfan parish, near the site of a former chapel. Services are held each Sunday and there is a thriving Sunday school. The Baptist chapel, closed in the 1930s, was a school canteen during the Second World War and is now a farm building.

Erected in 1925 the village hall stands on land given by the Sir Watkin of that time. He also provided most of the timber and opened the first fund raising effort, a sale of work which raised £100. Villagers had met several nights a week beforehand preparing goods for the sale.

The day after the Second World War broke out, WI and WVS members were in the hall to feed evacuees from Liverpool. Most of these returned home saying they would rather risk bombs than stay in such a far away place! Every returning serviceman had a 'welcome home' supper in the hall, a problem in rationing days, but the WI and WVS coped.

At a spot called Teacher's Field only a few stones remain of the old house of Caermynach, said to have been built mainly of wood. It belonged to Strata Marcella Abbey and was burnt during the Reformation. After the Dissolution of the Monasteries in the 16th century it became the property of the Vaughans of Llwydiarth. There are also the remains of a completely round building. Melindwr, on the opposite bank of the river was the monks' working mill and lower down river is Rhyd yr Abbadau, Monks' Ford, used before the bridge was built. Fachwen Ganol is the only house in the parish which is oblong, reminiscent of the type of house which comprised barn and dwelling, with access to the byre from the living quarters. The tall chimneys are said to have been built to stop the Red Men of the Dusk from entering down the chimney!

There are standing stones 4,000 years old in the forest, thought to have been used as a calendar with the help of a sighting stone to aid the planting and harvesting of crops. Beddau Cewri on Allt Boeth were said to be giants' graves but, in fact, are late medieval artificial rabbit warrens.

Village sports day has been held since the 1920s. Now, on Spring Bank Holiday, it is smaller than formerly – no more pony races – but the tradition of a tea party for the children continues.

There are two caravan parks, several holiday cottages and visitors join happily in village functions. A petrol station adjoins the shop, there is soon to be a car park and the mobile library calls every three weeks.

Time was when the mobile butcher and carrier each used a pony and cart, the butcher continuing until the Second World War. Then, in the 1950s, when the present family took over the post office – still open full time – farmers'

135

wives walked miles to sell eggs and butter to the dealer and visit the shop to spend the money. Not that they needed much, as they were nearly self-supporting. But they worked hard in the home and in helping on the land, so enjoyed a chat at the shop – as they still do with the same family there today!

Machynlleth

Machynlleth stands at the head of the estuary of the river Dyfi. The name comes from 'maen', which means stone block or pointer stone, and 'cynlleth', which means wetness and probably refers to the river. A stone bridge which cost £250 in 1805 crosses the river, successor to a wooden bridge.

The river Dyfi is noted for its salmon and sea trout and, well into the 20th century, poaching was an age-old tradition. Dyfi Fisheries Ltd now control the rights to fish the river, and issue licences for a fee.

Machynlleth began to grow when, in the 13th century, it was given the right to hold a market every Wednesday and two fairs every year. It became an important market centre and farmers from the countryside around would come, as they do today, to sell their sheep and cattle.

In 1863 the coming of the steam railway between Newtown and Machynlleth brought great changes. Formerly, everything people needed was made here or brought by boat to the port at Derwenlas, but with the coming of the railway, goods could be brought from other parts of the country by train. This meant the local craftsmen who made leather goods, iron tools and woollen cloth had very little work, and gradually the number of smiths, tanners, tailors and wool manufacturers fell.

Penrallt Street, Pentrehedyn Street and Maengwyn Street are the main thoroughfares and at the point where they all meet stands a clock tower built by the local people to celebrate the 21st birthday of Viscount Castlereagh, eldest son of the 5th Marquess of Londonderry. The tower is 78 feet high and stands on the site of the old town hall.

The Londonderry family were wealthy and important landowners in the Dyfi valley and lived at the mansion called Plas Machynlleth. Part of the house was built in 1653, the front in 1853. Many famous people came to visit the Plas, King Edward VII and Queen Alexandra, King George V and Queen Mary and also Lord Randolph Churchill. In 1948 the Plas was given to the town and has now been made into offices and the Council Chamber. The grounds have become a public park, where sheep-dog trials are held every year, at which the standard of performance is invariably high, both for dogs and men.

In Maengwyn Street stands the Parliament House and the Owain Glyndwr Institute. Near here Owain Glyndwr was proclaimed Prince of Wales in 1404, the last Prince of Wales to rebel against the English. Parliament House is a medieval Welsh town house built in the 16th century on the site where Owain Glyndwr held a parliament. The Owain Glyndwr Institute was built in 1911 and was made to look older than it is to match the Parliament House.

In the Institute there are large slabs of slate which used to hang in Pentrehedyn Street and Doll Street. These are 'toll stones' and list the tolls taken at the markets and fairs and at the two tollgates into Machynlleth. A toll had to be paid if one wanted to buy or sell produce in the market or take animals through. The money from the tolls was used, amongst other things, to mend the roads.

On the corner where Garsiwn Lane and Penrallt Street meet stands the 14th century Royal House, the oldest building in Machynlleth and, except for the Parliament House, the only medieval house in the town. Local tradition says that Dafydd Gam, who tried to assassinate Owain Glyndwr

137

during his crowning as Prince of Wales, was imprisoned there in 1404. The house, which is now a shop, was given the name of Royal House because King Charles I stayed there in 1644. It has always been thought that there is an underground passage from there to the river but one has never been found.

At the end of Maengwyn Street stands the Mayor's House, where the lord of the manor of Machynlleth lived in the 17th century. On the front of the house '1628 Owen Pugh uxor' is written, which means the house was owned by Owen Pugh and his wife.

Today employment for Machynlleth inhabitants is mainly in British Telecom, British Rail, forestry and farming. There is also an industrial estate with light engineering and a Laura Ashley factory. And one must not forget it was in Machynlleth that the first Laura Ashley shop was opened.

Meifod 🌿

> Who hath seen the territory fair
> Of Smiling Meifod, shall not see the like
> Nor tho' his life till Doomsday be prolonged
> > > Cynddelw, 12th Century poet, trans:

Meifod is on the move. In the 1980s the village saw many changes – new houses, new faces, a fine new village hall, and, most recently, the establishment of a centre for opera in Mid Wales.

But the past is ever-present. Dyffryn Hill dominates the village, and bears a series of wells said never to run dry, a hill fort dating from 300 BC and, it is believed, the sepulchre of Gwyddfarch, founder of Meifod's first church.

East of the village is Cobham's Garden, a field where Sir John Oldcastle, Lord Cobham, a leading Lollard, was cap-

The churchyard at Meifod

tured. From there he was taken to London and burned for his beliefs. He had previously escaped from the Tower and is said to have hidden for four years at Trefnanney, near Meifod, and in a chimney at Pantmawr Farm.

In the woods is a healing well, supposedly associated with the old saints of Meifod, and being restored as a tourist attraction.

Meifod's history includes strong associations with the Princes of Powys, some of whom are buried here. One, Madog, supported England's Henry II, but was assassinated at his wife's instigation. The palace of the princes was at Mathrafal, two miles out of the village, now merely a mound of earth shaded by trees.

The church of St Mary and St Tysilio stands back from the village street, behind fine trees, and is the last of three on the site. Gwyddfarch, a missionary, founded the first church in AD 550. The second, AD 728, was dedicated to St Tysilio, son of a Prince of Powys, and Prince Madog founded the third in 1170 and dedicated it to St Mary.

Surviving from the original church of St Mary are two Norman arches, but the main body of the present church is Tudor. It is thought that St Tysilio's church was built of wood.

Gargoyles on the tower, probably built about 1450, are an attractive feature and inside there is a carved Celtic cross on a stone coffin lid, an ancient font and six heraldic shields made of glass and dating from the 19th century. The organ case is of Gothic design.

David Evans, of Newtown, who produced stained glass for other Montgomeryshire churches, was responsible for some of that at Meifod.

The churchyard holds one mystery – the 'pirate's grave', marked only with a skull and crossbones.

The village lies at an angle between Oswestry in England and Welshpool in Wales and its name, some say, means middle or halfway dwelling. Or, so say others, it means summer dwelling, from being a summer residence of the Princes of Powys.

It seems to be just one long street in which two chapels, three garages, three shops, a bank and inn mingle with private dwellings. This pleasant, unassuming facade caters for a parish covering 13,000 acres, mainly agricultural. The village school and community hall and a fuel distribution depot are sited off-street, as are the public toilets. A piece in the *Daily Mirror* in 1971 described the cleanliness of these as 'at least equal to those of a first class hotel'.

Established architecture is varied, with good examples of Severn valley black and white, Georgian and Regency styles. On the village's western edge is Plas Dyffryn, for many years the home of Liberal leader Clement Davies; to the east is

Coed-y-Maen Hall, built in 1862 for Charles Watkin Williams Wynn, Conservative MP, and still occupied by a branch of the family.

The river Vyrnwy divides Meifod into two unequal parts. Flooding was common until a few years ago when streams were diverted and the problem alleviated. That same river is beloved by fishermen – and by kingfishers, the beauty of the latter to be seen among the varied wildlife on the river bank. There is much to do in the village besides fishing. There is a wealth of clubs to suit all tastes and a Cymdeithas Cymraeg which holds meetings alternately in Meifod and neighbouring Pontrobert.

Until recently most activities centred round the picturesque village institute in the main street, where parking became a hazard. Now the splendid new hall, provided partly by grants and partly through tremendous fund raising by the villagers, gives the sense of togetherness to carry the community into the 21st century.

Middletown 🪶

In 1983 a nightingale sang in Middletown. For the first time one nested on Moel y Golfa, one of the Breidden Hills overlooking the village. Its song brought enormous pleasure and was recorded on tape by many people.

Middletown itself stands on the A458 road, just inside Wales, on the south-facing slopes of Middletown Hill.

Earlier this century a tollgate barred the road where it crosses the England–Wales border. One can imagine the chaos this would cause in today's increased traffic. To make the village safer a 30 mph speed restriction sign was erected, but with little effect and crossing the road remains hazardous.

The Breidden Hotel lies on one corner of a 'staggered' crossroads at the village centre. Behind this is a residential caravan park and the village hall, the latter used regularly for gatherings of all kinds. The closure of the post office and store in 1988, and its conversion to a steak bar, decreased the number of shops, but there is still a small grocer's, a coal merchant and a garage and service station combined with a shop selling sweets, newspapers and gifts. However, the market town of Welshpool is only six miles away and, in spite of drastic cuts, there is still a reasonable bus service.

Middletown's original school was built in the mid-19th century, on the hillside above the village. Stone-built, its one upstairs room housed the pupils and was known as 'The College'. The ground floor room, called The Counting House, was used as a pay office for the local spar miners. Old ordnance maps show a network of footpaths, many converging on this small building, telling of the days when children attending school had to walk miles from over the hill or from cottages and farms to the south of the village.

Most of these farms reared cattle, pigs, sheep and poultry, as they do today, though the dairy herds are larger and require larger and more modern buildings.

When Middletown had its own railway station, known as Breidden, passengers had to take the narrow lane leading south from the crossroads in the village, passing on their way groups of old and more modern dwellings in an area known locally as Bumbletown. Then they had to turn off the road and cut across a field to the station. Both station house and platform have been demolished.

In the 1960s an epidemic of foot and mouth disease spread like wildfire through Shropshire and eastern Montgomeryshire. The nearest outbreak to Middletown, and one of the last, was just across the border at Plas y Court, near enough for one to see the flames rising from the burning carcases and smell the smoke as it drifted over the village. For weeks farmers were isolated from the outside world, unable to leave their farms for fear of spreading the disease. In order to

142

disinfect the tyres of vehicles 'dips' were built across many main roads, one being in Middletown itself.

Twice, over 20 years, the village was mentioned in a Sunday newspaper. First, a local girl fell in love with a wealthy Scottish laird. News of this reached the Press and the couple's every movement was written about. The laird beat a hasty retreat to his Scottish castle!

Then, in the spring of 1964, there was great excitement when Land Rovers and vans were seen going up and down the steep hill track. It was rumoured that two gipsy brothers were erecting a stone monument on top of Moel y Golfa in memory of a gipsy king. It all sounded rather far-fetched, but proved true when the story was published. In 1988 the ashes of another gipsy were buried up there, with all the attendant ceremony, and laying of wreaths around the monument.

Since the closure of the chapel, built in 1885, All Saints church has been the only place of worship in the village. It is built of local stone and blends well with the surrounding countryside.

Opposite the Breidden Hotel a narrow road climbs the south side of Middletown Hill, passing a council housing estate and some private houses before continuing through a gateway on to the hill itself. Near here, on the adjoining slopes of Moel y Golfa, the nightingale nested. To reach the summit of Middletown Hill one must follow one of many footpaths through the bracken. The climb is steep but the views from the top make it well worth the effort.

With an outlook like this it is not surprising that many years ago a fortress was built there, the remains of which are still clearly visible. Legend has it that in AD 50 Caradoc made his last stand against the Romans on this very spot, although this is a claim made for other locations as well. What would he have thought of the brightly coloured hang gliders that now, on calm, sunny days, soar around the summit looking like great butterflies?

Mochdre 🌿

Over the centuries the name Mochdre has been spelled variously as Mochdref, Moughtre and Moughtrey. Opinion is divided as to its origin and meaning. Using the Welsh word 'moch' in one sense, Mochdre would mean a precipitous or sloping township, which is in keeping with its natural configuration. But perhaps the more popular meaning derives from 'moch' meaning pig. There is a medieval story concerning a legendary Pryderi and Gwydion driving their pigs across Wales and their night-time stopping place 'between Kerry and Arwistli' became known as Mochdre.

The village lies three miles south-west of Newtown and the parish covers over 5,000 acres. A proportion of the population of 350 is still dependent on farming, mainly sheep and cattle, for its livelihood. As in many other rural areas, small farms are being amalgamated as they come on the market. Consequently, the number of people involved in farming is declining as the size of farms increases.

Side by side with this decline, however, housing in Mochdre has risen dramatically over the last 20 years. The hamlet of Stepaside, just nine cottages right through the 19th century, now has some 35 houses. As it is within easy commuting distance of Newtown this has benefited the community and has led to a return to the countryside of young families. The local school closed in 1968, owing to lack of pupils at that time, and today's children travel into Newtown for schooling.

Most adults work in Newtown, but there are a number of cottage crafts and country industries in Mochdre. These include upholstery and soft furnishing, doll making, dried flower crafts, painting and decorating, specialists in wedding, christening and birthday cakes, garden furniture, building site excavators, electrical contractors, and even a dental studio. There is also bed and breakfast accommodation and a caravan park.

Three churches, Anglican, Methodist and Baptist, still flourish and there is a post office at Cae Colley and one public house, the Dolau Inn. The old school is now the community centre, mainly used by the Young Farmers' Club, the Women's Institute, the Mothers' Union and the Parish Community Council, but available for any local event.

All Saints parish church is famous for its precious medieval wood carvings of Our Lord and the Blessed Virgin. They were found concealed on top of the wall plate during the restoration of the church in 1867 and had presumably been hidden there during the Reformation in the 16th century. Apart from their beauty these figures are of exceptional interest on account of their rarity value, only two having survived destruction in the time of Henry VIII. These unique treasures from the Middle Ages are now in the care of the National Museum of Wales in Cardiff.

As well as attracting people to come and live in the area, the beautiful natural scenery has always been an important factor in the livelihood of Mochdre's inhabitants.

The abundance of water flowing through the brooks on its way to the river Severn has provided scope for both work and leisure. Mochdre reservoir supplied Newtown and adjoining districts with a supply of pure water from 1872 until 1960. Now, re-named Lake Mochdre, it is a thriving commercial trout farm which produces fresh trout daily of well-known excellence.

In the 19th century the brooks provided the power for a number of mills, both corn and wool. Mochdre had one of the two last working woollen mills in Montgomeryshire. Known as the Red Factory, and tenanted and later owned by the Leach family, it ceased to exist in 1963.

So, whether known as Sloping Town or Pig Town, Moch-dre remains a busy and happy community and one which is proud of its long history.

Montgomery ❧

Montgomery, the county town of Montgomeryshire, has a population of about 1,000. It is a small town (it was the smallest borough in Wales prior to reorganisation in 1974). It is situated one mile from a length of the famous Offa's Dyke.

The first charter was dated 1227 and granted a market day and various fairs – only the May Fair is now held in the Broad Street.

Montgomery Castle, set on a rocky promontory on the western side of the town, was built between 1223–1227. From this position one is able to enjoy a panoramic view stretching from the Severn valley to the edge of the Shropshire plain. On a number of occasions in recent years the castle has been the site for open air concerts and during the festivals was illuminated, to the delight of residents and visitors.

Historically the oldest fortress site is the Iron Age hill fort 'Ffrydd Faldwyn', but little is known about it, although there was a small excavation earlier this century.

Another site of interest is Hendomen, a motte and bailey castle of the Norman period, and the first Montgomery castle. Excavations have been carried out here every July over 20 years and many of the finds can be seen at The Old Bell.

The 13th century parish church has many items of interest. The 15th century screen (the original is the western portion) has five open panels with traceried heads on either side of the doorway; the oak panels at the base are of a much later date. The rood loft is thought to have been made up from a pulpit of the mother church at Chirbury. The canopied tomb is of the Herbert family.

The Robber's Grave and the Policeman's Grave are in the churchyard. The story is that John Davies was hanged in 1821 having been found guilty of sheep stealing. At his trial he protested his innocence, stating that no grass would grow on his grave for 100 years, and according to records, this happened. The Policeman's Grave records the death of Constable William Davies in 1902 – carved on the gravestone are a policeman's helmet, lantern, truncheon and belt.

Montgomery was originally a walled town with four gates – Arthur, Cedewain, Chirbury and Ceri. Remains of the walls are still visible in parts of the town.

The town war memorial Garden of Remembrance is on the site of the old pound. The county war memorial, on the summit of the Town Hill, can be seen for miles. The walk to the memorial takes 30 minutes and from there the views are magnificent – Lymore Park, Corndon Hill, the Stiperstones, Kerry Hills, the Berwyns – whichever way one looks one cannot but be overwhelmed by the scenery.

Lymore Hall, situated in Lymore Park, was one of the largest black and white houses built on the Border. Regrettably, in 1930 it was demolished, but a photographic record is kept at the local museum.

The Town Council consists of eleven members and is chaired by the town mayor who is elected annually. They are mainly responsible for the institute, the playing fields and the allotments; the town hall and council houses being administered by the District Council.

The area is mostly agricultural, but some years ago the council encouraged a small components factory to open in the town and this provides employment for many local residents.

During the 1980s the council entered Montgomery in the

Wales in Bloom Competition (under 2,000 population) and, together with local people, made great efforts to decorate the town – being placed second on two occasions.

From 1728 to 1832 the Borough Member of Parliament was elected by the burgesses (or freemen) of Montgomery. The rights of the burgesses are hereditary and they were responsible for all affairs of the town until 1885 when the government of the borough was vested in the elected council. The direct male descendants, although they have no duties, still retain possession of the lands granted to the original freemen in the early charters and from which they derive an annual income.

Montgomery is a very active community. Over the years it has organised many festivals and large fund raising events, such as the 750th Charter Anniversary in 1977, when His Royal Highness The Prince of Wales was installed as an Honorary Freeman of the town. This was followed by festivals commemorating the Battle of Montgomery (1981), 'Cestyll '83', and the 450th Anniversary of the Formation of the Welsh Shires (1985).

The Civic Society, formed during the 1970s, restored – with help from funds raised during the Charter Celebrations – a 16th century house in Arthur Street, now known as The Old Bell, and many of the town's artefacts are displayed there. Plaques describing the town's history are affixed to many buildings in the town, receiving a Prince of Wales Award in 1980.

Visitors are made very welcome, with parking highly informal. Montgomery has changed very little over the years. Council and private building has not encroached upon the town to any great extent, so it remains unspoilt. It is becoming a 'must' for tourists, especially those who delight in walking and sight-seeing, and is an ideal base for visiting Mid Wales.

'Of all the Welsh Towns I have seen
Fair Montgomery is the Queen
In quiet peace she nestles there
Where folk have time to stand and stare
Mad world! you seem to pass her by
As in your noisesome car you fly.'

(Rev W. H. Middleton, Minister, Wesleyan church,
Welshpool, 1977)

New Mills & Manafon ❧

Visitors and residents who enjoy driving along the scenic
Rhiw valley should be grateful to all those who opposed
Liverpool Corporation's plans when they were considering,
in 1889 and again in 1966, the flooding of the valley for use
as a reservoir. The small villages of New Mills, Manafon and
The Green in the parish of Manafon would have been lost
and all the interesting facts of other lives and past years
would have been gone for ever, with no markers to remember them by.

Even so, in the 1981 census the population of the parish
was half what it was in 1847, when there were 795 people,
half of them speaking English. Over 60 of their houses have.
gone, but have been replaced by 37 new ones, built along the
valley since the 1930s.

In the 19th century New Mills had two inns, which were
located at the junction of two busy roads. They were frequented by hauliers and drovers, who used to leave their
stock in nearby fields whilst seeking refreshment or rest in
one of the inns. But with the construction of the Llanfair
light railway, New Mills ceased to be a focal point for this
trade. The resulting decline in trade caused both inns to close

prior to 1920. One became a guest house, shop and post office; the other, across the road, became private dwellings.

The energy from the Rhiw has provided power for woollen and corn mills over many years. At Bronhafon mill, owned by the same family for generations, there was also a kiln for drying oats. The 'New Mills' refers to the advanced design of the mill rather than to its age. At Dwyrhiew Mills factory accommodation housed 20 people, in addition to the miller's family.

The chapel in New Mills was built in 1825 and rebuilt in 1882, and although the work was being done for a religious organisation, the old tradition of supplying beer to the builders was observed during the restoration.

The village hall, which was erected soon after the First World War, has been, and still is, essential for parish activities. It was used as a school for Second World War evacuees.

An unusual addition to New Mills has been the formation of a Greek orthodox monastery at Mynachdy Sant Elias, formerly an old farmhouse. The monastery was established in 1973 by Father Barnabas. Weddings, baptisms and funerals have been held there and the various monastery bells can be heard in the valley.

A plaque on the wall of Sunnyside records that John Pugh of the Forward Religious Movement was born there in 1846.

One of the local mysteries is the exact location of 'the lions' grave'. Two circus lions were drowned when their cage overturned into the river whilst crossing the ford behind the post office.

Manafon school was completed in 1833 on land with a 99 year lease, donated by Mr Joseph Hays Lyon. The present building was begun in 1883 and completed in March 1884. Mr Rees Parry was headmaster there from 1923 to 1939 and his pupils achieved outstanding success, especially in competition with larger schools. Highlights for schoolchildren during the hard times of the 1930s were Sunday school outings to the coast, and Christmas tea parties, when everyone was given a present of a good book. All this was due to the generosity of the Davies family of Gregynog.

There has been a church at Manafon since at least 1254, but the church as it is known today has been restored many times over the years. The last time was in 1898, when a medieval holy water stoup was found. This is now located to the right-hand side of the main door. When the new floor was laid it was found that burials had taken place inside the church.

Rectors of fame from Manafon include Walter Davies, remembered for his three volumes on *The State of Agriculture and Economy in Wales*, published in 1810 and 1814; William Morgan, an eminent Welsh poet whose bardic name was Penfro and the Rev R. S. Thomas, rector 1942–54, who became a famous poet. His wife, Mildred Eldridge, is equally well known as a painter and illustrator of children's books. The wall mural in the nurses' dining room at Gobowen Hospital is an example of her work.

The smithy was worked until 1958 and belonged to the same family for 200 years.

The Beehive is the only inn left of five that used to be in the parish. The Green Tavern at Peacevale in The Green was closed prior to 1851.

There was also a chapel at The Green, situated on the corner to Llwyn-Copa, but all that remains today is a short stretch of railings.

Holidaymakers have a choice of two caravan parks in the area, at the Gwernydd and at The Moat.

Newchapel 🐝

Newchapel, near Llanidloes, is not a village in the true sense of the word. The Baptist chapel is the place where people of the area come together on Sundays for worship.

In 1740 Baptists and Independents established a chapel here, the earliest Nonconformist building of any denomination in the locality. Very soon the Baptists were in sole charge. In 1815 the chapel was rebuilt, and it was restored in 1905. It was burned down in 1954, leaving only the walls standing, but was rebuilt and opened again for worship in May 1957. During the three years it took to rebuild, people went to other chapels. Sunday school was held at Prospect Farm.

Two cottages once stood in what is now part of the graveyard, in the corner between the road leading to Pen-y-Banc and the road which passes in front of the chapel. They were demolished in about the 1920s and some years later an old lady who had lived in one of them was buried on the site of what had once been her kitchen.

Of three other cottages across the road from the chapel, two are now converted into one dwelling, the third is vacant.

Highlights of the year are the anniversary services which have been held in the chapel for many years. These are well attended by people who enjoy being entertained and joining with adults and children in giving praise to God. Much hard work goes into learning songs and recitations by people willing to give their time and talent to bring pleasure to others.

There are a number of old lead mine workings in the district, at Cwm-mawr, at Gorn and in the valley below Cwm. A small reservoir was constructed in the Bradnant brook to provide water to wash the lead as it was brought out of the workings in the valley. Here traces of a little cottage can still be seen. The people who lived there made their own bread by making the dough and carrying it up the fields to be baked in an oven at Cwm.

Years ago there were many more houses around the area. Most have now gone, though the remains of one at Cefn Hafod are still visible. At Upper Esgair a big new house has been built on the site of an old one; a black and white house, uninhabited, stands by the road from Newchapel to Dolwen and another empty cottage stands at the bottom of the wood below Upper Esgair.

Before the coming of the school bus, children had to walk long distances to school at Oakley Park, Llidiartywaen or Llanidloes.

Newchapel is first and foremost a farming community. Before the Second World War most of the men worked at home or on other farms and most girls worked as house-maids or the like. Nowadays, farms are more mechanised so do not require so many workmen. Young people find work elsewhere, in factories or offices or go further away to places where work is more plentiful.

Newtown ✤

Newtown, the largest community in the old county of Mont-gomeryshire, was a new town in the 14th century. Roger de Mortimer was granted the right to hold a weekly market and two fairs a year there, in return for helping Edward I to take Dolforwyn Castle, the ruins of which lie to the north of the town. The name took on a new meaning in the 1970s when it became an area of major development, designated as the centre of new growth in Mid Wales.

The Romans regarded Caersws, five miles to the south, as a better site but by 1277, when Edward I invaded Wales, there was a scattered township on either side of the river Severn in the area then known as Llanfair-yng-Nghedewain (St Mary in Cedewain). The remains of a mound on the site of a Norman fort are still to be seen not far from the town centre. By the end of the 14th century the new town had become a borough with its own charter.

Museums and buildings in the town reflect Newtown's history. In the 18th century, it became the centre of a flourishing woollen industry and a major producer of Welsh flannel. The Georgian buildings which can still be seen date from this period of prosperity, while one of the old hand-weaving buildings in Commercial Road was opened as a textile museum in 1967.

Newtown boasts the only department store in Montgomeryshire. This was opened by Pryce Jones, who supplied Welsh flannel to Queen Victoria and who pioneered the mail order business, a fact which no doubt accounts for the site of the building, completed in 1879 and still in use today, near the railway station. Goods were sent to all parts of the world and the trade was so great that three luggage compartments were reserved each day on the train from Newtown to Euston.

Sir Pryce Pryce-Jones, as he became, was responsible for bringing one of Newtown's most interesting buildings to its tucked-away place in Milford Road. This is a small 15th century timber and stone hall, brought from Dolgellau in 1885. It was thought at one time to have been used for a parliament called by Owain Glyndwr in Dolgellau in 1404, but is now known to have been the home of Lewis Owen, a Baron of the Exchequer, murdered in 1555. These days it is used as a Quaker meeting house.

Newtown's most famous son is Robert Owen, who was born in a house in Broad Street in 1771, but who spent most of his life elsewhere, notably in New Lanark in Scotland. There he developed the philanthropic ideas which gained him fame as a social reformer with a particular interest in education and social welfare, because of all that he did to improve living and working conditions for children and for women. He returned to Newtown to die and is commemorated by a museum in the old town library not far from the spot where he was born, by a statue and by a memorial in the remains of St Mary's church near the river.

There is also a small museum of national significance. In 1978, W H Smith decided to restore their Newtown shop to its original state, as it was when it opened in 1927. The shop itself provides a nostalgic treat for those older visitors who can remember the W H Smith shops of the 1930s and 1940s, with their oak furnishings, high bookcases, some glass-fronted, and tables, while upstairs a small display shows the history of this world famous store from its beginnings in 1792.

Today, in the late 1980s, Newtown is returning to the prosperity it enjoyed nearly 200 years ago when the woollen industry flourished. It is well-sited, lying on two major north–south trunk roads and on the main railway line from Aberystwyth to London. The final stretch of the Mont-gomery Canal, which used to terminate in a port at Newtown, has unfortunately been filled in and only a floodbank marks the site, but the river Severn still winds through the town. In the past, the town has suffered from severe flooding – St Mary's church was abandoned in the early 19th century for this reason – but today embankments built along the town section of the river, and the Clwyedog dam upstream, con-trolling the level of the water, prevent this.

The town is an important industrial and cultural centre. New industrial estates and a Science Park have encouraged firms to move to the town and housing has been provided for incoming workers. There are regular art and craft exhibi-tions in the modern Davies Memorial Gallery, the bequest of Margaret Davies of Gregynog who, with her sister, was a liberal patron of the arts. The Theatre Hafren, attached to the Montgomeryshire College of Further Education, pro-vides a high quality environment for performances by visit-ing orchestras and theatre and ballet companies as well as for the Montgomeryshire WI Drama Festival, held there each year, an important event in the WI calendar.

Penegoes 🦜

Penegoes is approached from Machynlleth by an old bridge, Felin Gerrig (Millstone), on a road said to date from Roman times. This is supported by the name of a group of cottages on the outskirts of Penegoes, Craig yr Henffordd (Stone of the Old Street).

To the left stands the old mansion of Gallt y Llan, half-way up the hill of the Gallt (Wooded Hill). Legend says that the nearby mansion of Dolguog (Fastness Field) is connected with the vanished fortress of the ruler Owain Cyfeiliog, in his day recognised as Prince of Powys. He died in 1197 and is remembered as a poet and administrator. He introduced sheep farming, still a vital industry in the district.

Broad approaches up the hill of Gallt y Llan can still be seen. The site is of strategic importance, commanding a view of the approaches through the narrow valley from Corris, the passage from Mathafarn and the routes from the five summits of Plynlimon.

The name Penegoes means Head of Egeos, Egeos being a Celtic saint whose head is said to be buried beneath the grove of oaks which still stand a few yards beyond the church. Tradition says death and pestilence would strike anyone disturbing it.

On the southern side of the road, nearly opposite the church, is a mineral well said to have healing properties. This has recently been restored to its original condition and is being visited once more.

The old rectory is famous as the birthplace of the land-scape painter Richard Wilson (1714–1782). A frequent visitor at a later date to the old rectory was Liverpool-born poet

156

and authoress Felicia Dorothea Hemans (1793–1835). Mrs Hemans wrote the poem *Casabianca*, with the famous line 'The boy stood on the burning deck'. Her brother-in-law was rector of Penegoes and she spent much of her time there.

On the banks of the River Crewi stands the completely restored 17th century water-mill. At Felin Crewi they still use the original burr stones which are driven slowly by the power of the river. This traditional milling process retains all the flavour and valuable nourishment of the natural vitamins, protein and dietary fibre of the whole grain. Originally, local farmers brought their corn to be ground. The miller would be paid a percentage of the corn or he would barter his skill for other goods or services which he needed. Today, clean, British-grown wheat suitable for milling is bought in and stored in a silo by the old barn. A great variety of flour, wheatgerm, bran and muesli can be bought at the mill, which also caters for hungry visitors.

Pennant 🪢

In a secluded valley some two miles west of Llangynog is the hamlet of Pennant. Once a village of 200 people, it now consists only of the church of St Melangell, a few houses and a legend.

Melangell, the legend says, was a princess who fled from Ireland in the 7th century and sought sanctuary in a cave above the church, where she gave shelter to the birds and animals of the valley. One day Brochwel, a Prince of Powys, came across her sheltering a hare from his hounds and he later declared the valley a protected area.

Surrounded by a circular wall with a lychgate, the church has a shrine to St Melangell. A recent survey established the site of a cockpit outside the churchyard.

As it is reputed to be haunted, local people will not go near the church after dark.

Penrhos, Sarnau & Deytheur 🦜

Penrhos, Sarnau and Deytheur share a church, chapels, Women's Institute, post office and annual sports, and the fact that they have no shop or bus service.

Until 1950, however, Penrhos and Sarnau had 'John's Bus'. This was a Model T Ford, owned by John Jones, a one-legged man, and it ran bi-weekly on market days – to Welshpool on Monday and Oswestry on Wednesday. Crosville took over until the 1970s, when they stopped through lack of passengers. John's Bus was retired to Beaulieu Motor Museum but is now privately owned and to be seen at steam rallies.

Penrhos church was built in 1845 on the site of an earlier church of 1625, built partly at the expense of Hugh Derwas of Penrhos Hall. The first church, dedicated to the Holy Trinity, was a small building made of rubble stone with mud plaster and a roof of shingle or boards. Communion was given in the pews. The earliest registers of 1695 were written on loose sheets of paper, so some are lost. It stood for 219 years as a chapel of ease to Llandrinio church and in 1844 was constituted a new Ecclesiastical District, consolidated with four adjoining parishes.

Penrhos Hall, of which there is now no trace, was a large black and white mansion in fields south of the church, and the home of the Derwas family for 200 years. John ap Owen, who took his grandmother's name, Derwas, was the first to live at the hall, which he probably built in the 16th century. He could claim a distinguished lineage, one of his ancestor's being a lord of Nannau, Esquire of the Body to Henry VI.

A Derwas descendant, looking at the house in the late

1800s, found it in bad condition but described it as one of the 'most picturesque desolate houses'. The family now own ironmongers' shops in Oswestry and Welshpool.

The village school, built by local subscription on land given by the then lord of the manor, Lord Harlech, opened in 1902. A simple red-brick building, it was divided by a curtain into two classrooms with an open fire at each end. Later, these were changed to coke-burning stoves and the caretaker, Mrs Wygold, cycled from Sarnau every night around midnight to stoke them. When the kitchen was added during the Second World War Mrs Wygold became cook. She was a 'character', who is remembered with affection. The school closed in 1966 and was used as a village hall, but became rather neglected until in 1984 a committee was formed to run and renovate it. Refurbished, it was reopened by Alex Carlile, MP, and now takes its proper place as the centre of village activities.

There used to be a mill about a mile from the church, where farmers took corn to be ground – and sheep to be washed in the mill stream. At some time there was a brick-yard, now marked only by the name of a certain corner in the road. In the wood opposite the church, now owned by the Forestry Commission, there were three fishponds belonging to the hall. During the Second World War two planes collided in mid-air and came down in the wood. A guard was quickly posted to discourage souvenir hunters.

Sarnau, half a mile south of Penrhos, consists of a few houses, a United Reformed church, post office and outlying farms. Years ago each family had its own little business – baker, blacksmith, cobbler and so on. One farmer was proud father to eleven sons and five daughters, most of whom served in the forces during the Second World War. The eldest, now in her 80s, remembers the shoes the cobbler made for her to walk to school in Trefnanney, several miles away.

The third village, Deytheur, once had three inns. One, The Court House, was used for court sittings. A school was opened there in 1639 intended for boys of the Hundred of Deytheur. Later it was extended to take boarders, and closed in 1967. The Primitive Methodist chapel used to hold a camp meeting in June, the congregation sitting on benches to hear the preacher, who stood on a farm wagon.

The district's sports are held in a field at Deytheur on the first Saturday in June. There are races, games, a mini-show and tea, arrangements being made by a committee of people from all three communities.

Penrhos means 'the place at the head of the open heathland'. Penrhos church is open to the plain of Shropshire, the heart of England, the Fens, the great plains of Europe, and the steppes of faraway Russia!

Penstrowed 🌿

Penstrowed boasts the title of 'The Smallest Hamlet in Wales'. Covering an area of some 1,220 acres, it is situated on the outskirts of Newtown on the Newtown–Llanidloes road and is bounded by the villages of Mochdre and Caersws, separated from Aberhafesp by the river Severn.

Its most notable landmark is the church of St Gwrhais (St George), a saint of the Church of Deiniol. The church was founded in the 6th century and the remains of its founder are said to be buried in the churchyard. Seven later incumbents are also buried there.

The church itself is set back from the main road, behind the rectory. It is a small, single chamber building which was entirely rebuilt in 1863. The stained-glass windows were inserted in 1864. One of these depicts Christ appearing to the three Marys, and was placed there as a monument to John Herbert, a member of the parish.

Penstrowed Hall is another landmark situated on the Newtown–Llanidloes road. This is a large black and white farmhouse, built in the 16th century. It features an impressive oak staircase and oak beams throughout, and it has been inhabited for two generations by the Hughes family.

Farming in the area consists mainly of sheep and dairy cattle. Other industries within Penstrowed include quarrying and cement production. There is a working quarry which yields silica granite and is of great interest to archaeology students who visit from Sussex and Leicester Universities. A sample of the granite is displayed in Kensington Geological Museum in London. The quarry is a favourite site for conservationists, the habitat creating much interest.

Originally owned by Montgomery District Council, the quarry was purchased by Mr Bernard Corfield in the 1950s but at that time was not being worked. The new owner began business on a small scale with just two employees. The granite was drilled and blasted out and transported by rail to the main Newtown line. A cement manufacturer now leases property from the quarry owners. Neither industry is run on a large scale today, but each is valuable in its own right.

Lord David Davies, of Llandinam, was a great railway enthusiast, who also followed the hunt. It is said that on one occasion he was present when part of the line from the quarry to the main Newtown line was being laid. The huntsman's horn was heard, David Davies and the workmen downed tools and went after the fox!

A small chapel was available for use by the quarry workers. They erected the building themselves with materials from the quarry. This was done in their own time, and the men were paid in beer! As the quarry became redundant, the chapel was unused for some time. Because of its location and its permanent covering of dust from the quarry, it was unsuitable for leasing, and consequently it has been relegated to a storehouse.

In June 1936 a railway disaster was averted by a young woman, then Miss Bernice Haynes. Miss Haynes was brought up at Scofell station, where her mother was station mistress and her father a railway ganger.

On 20th June there had been a terrible thunderstorm, followed the next day by torrential rain and storms. Miss Haynes and her father went to look at the stone arched bridge over the Mochdre brook, just before its junction with the river Severn. The brook had burst its banks and masonry, trees, roots and, believe it or not, two cows still fastened to their stalls, came flooding down. Miss Haynes was warned by her father of the danger of standing on the bridge and promptly vacated it. Within minutes the bridge had gone, leaving only one set of railway lines suspended in mid-air.

Miss Haynes ran two miles into Newtown to raise the alarm. The signalman wasted no time, and was able to stop the next train going beyond Moat Lane station. Thus a railway disaster was averted. Miss Haynes, now Mrs Bernice Roberts, lives in Mochdre, overlooking the valley.

Plans have been drawn up for a new hotel in the hamlet, to be situated on the Newtown–Llanidloes road at the site of the old Penstrowed garage. It is to have 60 bedrooms, a leisure complex and conference facilities.

Penybontfawr

Penybontfawr is situated at the confluence of the rivers Tanat and Barrog, in the upper Tanat valley. In winter all is outwardly quiet, but summer brings a stream of visitors to the caravan sites, testifying to the popularity of the area with city dwellers, who love the steep hills rising sharply from the valley. Strangers entering from the east may be forgiven for thinking they have discovered a new star, but it is only the light of Cefn Ucha, which, at nearly 1,000 ft, has a magnificent view down the Tanat valley and far into Shropshire.

Like many villages, beneath its quiet exterior there is a hive of activity. The community centre, opened in 1973, is in constant use.

Pennant school, opened in 1971, replaced neighbouring Llangynog CP school and Penybontfawr Church in Wales school, which itself had taken in pupils from two smaller schools, Hirnant and Cwmdu on their closure. Originally built for 60 pupils, the numbers now exceed that, so, with a thriving Ysgol Feithrin, the future seems secure.

Pupils are taught Welsh and English alongside each other, which appears to work well, as all children, whether of Welsh or English parentage, are fluent in both languages by the time they leave.

The area is predominantly Welsh speaking, especially among the farming community, farming being the main occupation outside the village. Many village people also have farming connections, but during the 1980s there has been an influx from all walks of life, with several new dwellings being built. Structurally, the village centre has changed little, although in bygone days it possessed a milliner, cobbler, blacksmith, wheelwright, confectioner, butcher, and, in the old station yard, a coal merchant. Today there is one store incorporating the post office, a public house, fish and chip shop, cafe, garage, building enterprises and a small woodcraft business. A bowling green was made on the site of the demolished Memorial Hall, the war memorial plaques having been transferred to the community centre. One village pump remains, near Afallon, formerly known as Birch Oak, so called because a nearby birch and an oak tree grew intermingled.

Despite diminishing congregations, the Nonconformist chapels – Elim, Pen Nebo and Bethania – are still open for regular services, as is St Thomas' church, built in 1855. The

163

The harpist, Nansi Richards, of Penybontfawr

old graveyard is at the front of the church, with a new plot at the rear, consecrated in 1965.

One of the gravestones records the sad tale of the Foel Ortho family, father, mother and four children, aged 15 to 21, who died of black fever in 1863–64. Another is unusual in that its monument, although appearing similar to the others is, on closer inspection, found to be made of wood. It marks the resting place of two brothers, Henry and John Jones, who both died aged ten months, in 1884 and 1886 respectively. The memorial has withstood the test of time well, each word as clear as the day it was carved. By the hedge to the west is buried Robert Davies, who died in 1864 at the age of 29, reputed to be the last Montgomeryshire shingles 'charmer'. To qualify, the person or one of his ancestors, to the ninth generation, had to have partaken of eagle's flesh. The procedure of the cure was to spit on the affected area and chant a certain verse.

The Women's Institute produced a comprehensive survey of the graveyard in 1984, which is available for perusal, as is the Domesday Book, compiled in 1983.

Next to the church stands the old school, now owned and regularly used by Birmingham Scouts, as a base for outdoor pursuits.

Several famous names can be connected with the village by birth or other circumstance. Cynddelw, a 19th century bard, was born at Tynymeini, now derelict. Professor J. M. Davies, MA, Bala and Bangor Theological College, was born at Wernddu Fach in 1853. Ieuan Gwynedd opened a school at Bethania in 1839 with great success.

But surely the most famous name is that of Nansi Richards, Telynores Maldwyn, who died in 1979. The centenary of her birth at Penybont Farm was celebrated in May 1988, and two commemorative slate plaques unveiled, on the walls of her old home and at the community centre. When, at the age of 20, Nansi won the triple harp competition at Llangollen

National Eisteddfod against harpists of considerable renown, the bells of St Thomas' were rung amid great jubilation. Though widely travelled, she remained faithful to her home village, and unassuming in character. How delighted she was to receive a doctorate for her contribution to music! The Nansi Richards Fund awards an annual scholarship to enable a young harpist to receive expert tuition.

The main event of the year is the combined horticultural show and sheep-dog trials on August Bank Holiday weekend. Entries in the horticultural and produce section are always of a high standard, with a special section for caravan site visitors. The sheep-dog trials are held in a nearby field with continuous competition for a day and a half. There are also local sheep classes and both machine and hand-shearing competitions.

Love of music and culture is evident in the community and there is a wealth of talent. Penybontfawr Male Voice Choir, formed in 1951, are National Winners and regularly booked for concerts over a wide area. On the outskirts of the village the stone circle, Meini r Orsedd, still stands, as a reminder of a successful Powys Eisteddfod held in 1966.

Er pob newid a fu, neu a fydd yn y dyfodol, hyderwn y deil yr Iaith Gymraeg yn ein bro, mor gadarn a 'r hen bont a roddodd enw i'n pentref.

(Despite past and future changes, we trust that the Welsh language in our area will remain as firm as the bridge that gave the village its name.)

Pont Robert

Nestling in the hills of North Montgomeryshire, the village of Pont Robert is bisected by the river Vyrnwy and two miles from the nearest major road.

The village derives its name from Robert ap Oliver of

Cynhinfa, who was responsible for the rebuilding of the river bridge after the original had been swept away by floods in 1633. The ap Oliver family owned Dolfeiniog Mill nearby and it is thought the bridge was built for the convenience of transport to and from the premises. Local myth however, says that he erected the bridge to keep his feet dry when he visited his lady-love on the opposite bank!

Although small, the village was of great influence in early local industrial history. During the centuries it has boasted three grain mills, two iron forges and a woollen factory. Two of the mills have disappeared, together with one of the forges; the remaining mill has been converted into a modern residence and the shell of the woollen factory can still be seen. Evidence of another forge can be found at the Old Forge Mill on the opposite bank of the river from Dolobran Hall. The mill feeder can still be traced and evidence of clinker is found in its banks, together with the remains of the sluice gates.

The other iron foundries, Parc Mathrafal Forge, situated on the river Banwy, and Dolobran, or Ffridd Mathrafal Forge, near Dolobran Hall, were run by the Lloyds of Dolobran. The Lloyds, who still own the estate, have been at Dolobran since 1425. Among their family were Samson, founder of Lloyd's Bank and Stewart & Lloyds, ironfounders; and Thomas, friend of William Penn, who went to America and became Deputy Governor of Pennsylvania. The family followed the Quaker persuasion and Charles Lloyd was responsible for the building of the Dolobran meeting house in 1700. A school was run there for 13 years by John Kelsall, who later became clerk to Dolobran Forge and secretary to Charles Lloyd, and from whose unpublished diaries a lot of local history is gleaned. For 180 years the meeting house was disused, and the oak panelling and elders' gallery were stripped and shipped to America. In 1957 the chapel was once again open for worship.

In 1729 the Dolobran Forge was closed but reopened 60 years later as a woollen factory for the production of flannel, employing 100 people.

Many of the old buildings have survived. Near the bridge is Hendafarn, a drovers' inn, and the original school, both now converted into comfortable dwellings. Another is the old Methodist chapel built in 1800, at which John Hughes, the hymn writer, lived and preached; he is buried in the graveyard nearby. On the edge of the Dolobran estate is a 17th century half-timbered house, Garth Fawr.

On the northern outskirts lie eight acres of mature deciduous woodland, Coed Pendugm Reserve, given by deed of trust to the North Wales Naturalists' Trust by Mr Langshaw Rowlands and now administered by the Montgomeryshire Wildlife Trust. These woods contain remnants of ancient natural forest, together with a variety of wildlife and woodland flora.

At the southern edge of the village are 250 acres of coniferous forest, formerly part of Powis estate but now owned by the Forestry Commission. On this site are the remains of two ancient hill forts which would have commanded fine views of the Meifod valley. Evidence of a charcoal industry is still found within the forest, used in the iron smelting process.

Today the village boasts a community hall, primary school, public house, shop with post office, three chapels and a church in weekly use. Many clubs and organisations are based within the boundaries. The face of the village is changing. A main sewerage scheme is under construction, together with several new houses and the possibility of more to come. Although at present the main occupation of the inhabitants is connected with agriculture, this will probably diversify in the foreseeable future with the influx of newcomers to the village.

Sarn 🦢

Drive through Sarn on the A489 – there is the garage, the village school, the church, with the recreation ground opposite, the school and the pub, with the chapel tucked away at the back. But where are the houses? There are few. The three bungalows built in 1988 are enough to make a noticeable change.

A passing traveller does not see the maze of little lanes leading to houses grouped in ones and twos, tucked away in the hills. Many of these are half-timbered, their bones made of oak. Oak trees still flourish in hedgerows filled with the wild flowers which have vanished from other areas. Primroses, honeysuckle and wild roses all take their turn.

Most of the people come from farming families. The quiet, green hills are home to dairy and sheep farms and Montgomeryshire College of Further Education has its hill farm at Sarn. There are many smallholdings, created from larger farms after the First World War for those lucky enough to return.

There is forestry. Patches of conifers take their place in the landscape and do not dominate it.

True, there is no village shop nowadays, but, luckily, there is a post office for pensions, stamps – and gossip!

Sarn still has its village school, another blessing to count, 33 children keeping the playground alive. Usually one week in January the school is closed. When snow blocks the narrow lanes, the hills give a good impression of the Alps and children get out their sledges – or fertiliser sacks will do!

Once a Plymouth Brethren meeting house, the village hall now houses committee meetings, dances, WI, Young Farmers and Youth Club meetings, the harvest supper and the Christmas bazaar. There is usually something going on.

Sarn has the Lord Davies of the 1920s to thank for the

Sarn village

recreation ground. There one will find bowls – an addictive local passion, tennis, and Sunday League football matches. Children play on the swings and consign Guy Fawkes to the flames on bonfire night. Between times sheep act as groundsmen, trimming the grass.

Holy Trinity church was built in 1868, the Baptist chapel in 1827. During the year they come together for the United Remembrance Day Service and the Community Carol Service. For the latter all the village societies elect one poor soul to read a passage from the Bible. The relief when it is over for another year and the mince pies are served!

Every village round about has its agricultural show – but Sarn's is the best! It was started to celebrate victory in the First World War, slumped, along with so much else, during the Depression, and was revived to celebrate again – victory in the Second World War. The tent is crowded with the things which should be at such a show – cakes, pickles, knitting, patchwork, flowers, vegetables and the efforts of the children. So, on the second Saturday in August come to visit Sarn, and be sure to see also the stock and the dog show and the stalls. Then collapse in the WI tent for a really good tea!

Staylittle

Staylittle, or Penfforddlas, which means common at the top of the green road, is a lovely hamlet close to the head of the Llwyn Clywedog Reservoir, with its spectacular dam.

A blacksmith legend gave the hamlet its English name of Staylittle. It appears that two brothers, the local blacksmiths, took such pride in their skill and work that, without the restrictions of modern practices to govern their pace, the smiths could shoe horses so quickly that riders, and travellers on the stagecoaches, needed only to 'stay a little' before continuing their journeys.

Reminders of history abound, with several sites of bronze age tumuli in the area. A chalice was found when one was opened. In more recent times an important 11th century battle took place at Maesmedrisiol – the field of the three skulls. Today the site is a modern sheep farm, still bearing the name. A farm nearby, Dolbachog, was written of in Domesday Book. The present farmhouse stands on the site of the one mentioned and was once a Quaker Meeting House. Farther along the valley Esgairgoch has a Quaker yard – burial ground – within its boundaries.

The old drovers' road from the Star Inn at Dylife to Rhiwdyfeity is Roman in origin and passes through to Carno. The track may still be walked, and has tales abounding. Cattle and sheep were shoed for the long trek to market, sometimes having to walk as far as Maidstone in Kent. Geese and ducks had their feet coated in tar-pitch to enable them to walk the distances without injury. One tale tells of a young lad who, taking his geese to market, had diligently covered the feet of the birds. He had herded them some five or so miles along the lonely track when the geese, tired of this game, decided to fly home to their comfortable farmyard. He had forgotten to clip their wings!

The mighty Hafren Forest is a short distance from Stay-little, where picnic sites and woodland walks encourage the visitor and resident alike to linger and enjoy the quiet beauty of the flora and fauna that is the heartland of mid-Wales and to view the infant river Severn, from which the forest takes its name, Hafren being Welsh for Severn. The source of both mighty rivers Severn and Wye rise within a mile of each other on the nearby hills of Plynlimon.

Another river, Rheidol, also rises on Plynlimon, which reminds one of another legend – that of Father Plynlimon and his three lovely daughters – Severn, Wye and Rheidol. When he at last decided it was time for them to leave home he told them that he would give them all the land they could cover next day between dawn and dusk and between their home and the sea.

Severn awoke early, so slipped quietly away taking the longest way to the sea – that is why she winds so much. Wye awoke, found Severn had stolen a march on her and sighed, 'Ah, well, she's sure to have gone the longest way to the sea, but I will go the prettiest,' hence the beautiful course of the Wye. Rheidol overslept, knew she must hurry and would not get much land, so she took the shortest way – rapidly down to Aberystwyth.

Trefeglwys 🌺

The parish is bounded by the Lower Ffridd in the east; the old Cardiganshire border at the top of Plynlimon to the west; Waun Garno to the north and Llynebyr – lake – to the south. The ancient area of Arwystli, once the seat of the Lords of Powys, includes the parish of Trefeglwys.

Berthlas, a little known and rather fine example of a timber-framed farmhouse, circa 16th century, stands outside the village. In 1797 a Sunday school was held there and in 1803 a free school established, making Berthlas the real beginning of schooling in the lower parish.

Folk tales abound in this delightful corner of mid-Wales, although, sadly, many have been lost, as in so many previously remote corners of Wales. Fortunately, the poetic tradition of the Welsh people has kept alive some tales in verbal form, and for the collector of local legend there is much to be recorded still.

For instance, Talgarth, a very fine Elizabethan timber-framed house is at the site of the 'Hanging Tree'. Local tales tell of a Scots pine used as a gibbet, the pine being on the place once occupied by an ancient oak.

A locally well-known 'white witch' is reputed to have lived in a tiny one-up-and-one-down house in the woods above Llynebyr, the ruins of such a cottage can be seen in the woods. Llynebyr has its own legends and is a strangely beautiful, haunted place even now with its redwood trees and derelict boathouse.

Among some of the better known folk tales is the story of a shepherd and his wife with twin sons, who, in the wife's temporary absence, were strangely changed. They stopped growing and became ugly and cross tempered. The parents consulted the Wise Man of Llanidloes, who told the mother to prepare soup for the harvest supper in an eggshell. By listening to the twins' remarks she would know whether they were of human or faery understanding.

When she served the soup she heard one remark to the other:

> 'Acorn before oak I knew
> And egg before the hen,
> But I never heard of an eggshell brew
> As dinner for harvest men.'

This proved to her that the twins were indeed faery changelings, and they were thrown into the waters of Llyn-ebyr. The fairies arrived to take them from the lake and the real twins were restored to their parents.

Trefeglwys is becoming increasingly popular as a holiday area, and has much to offer the visitor. The immediate surroundings give access to a variety of countryside walking, from moorland and mountain to wooded valley. There is much for those whose interests are artistic, or in history, folklore, ancient buildings or the study of wildlife.

Trefnanney ✤

Trefnanney is not a village in the usual sense of the word, but a scattering of farms and cottages along and around the banks of the river Vyrnwy. 'Dwellings by the stream' is a rough translation.

In the 19th century there were varied occupations besides farming. There was a working mill at Pontyscowrhyd, on the bank of the river, until the end of the Second World War, but it fell into disrepair and the weir was washed away by floods in the winter of 1947. There was a late medieval cruck hall nearby, where John Mytton settled in the 16th century, founding the Welsh branch of this notable family. Sadly, this was demolished in 1956 to enlarge a farmyard close by. Early in this century a bridge was built across the river at this point with a tollgate and a new road from Pontyscowrhyd to Ystym Colwyn farm. The tollgate cottage is still inhabited and has been enlarged. The angling rights on the river used to belong to angling clubs over the Border, but more recently have been sold back to the farmers.

One farm is called Tanhouse Farm and has the remains of workers' cottages nearby, suggesting that there had once been a tannery there. Near to the present school are two cottages where for three generations lived a family among whose members were the local smith, wheelwright and carpenter. Well into the 1950s farmers were taking their horses there to be shod and carts to be repaired.

Before 1870 the local children went to a dame school at Hendre Hen, which is now used as a barn. There is a sad little story of a girl of seven, Elizabeth, an orphan who lived at a farmer's house working for her keep. One of her duties was to take the boy of the farm to school each day. His father was charged 1d per week for his son's education. Elizabeth enjoyed this chore and eagerly drank in all the lessons, until one day it was discovered that no-one was paying for her. She had to stop.

The present school, a primary school, was erected by Captain D. H. Mytton in 1870 when compulsory free education to the age of twelve was introduced. In 1896, it is noted, there were three untrained teachers and 110 pupils. Many of the children had to walk three to five miles each morning and evening. The older ones had many tasks, such as keeping the rooms clean, carrying water, gardening and emptying the earth closets.

In those days, although many of the children were Welsh-speaking, it was against the law to teach in Welsh. Now, of course, Welsh is a compulsory subject and, in spite of the many closures of village schools in the past few years, Trefnanney school has been largely modernised and is a lively, thriving unit with 32 pupils and two trained teachers.

Trefnanney Hall was a large red-brick house built about 1770. It was purchased by the Mytton family in the 19th century and tenanted – they owned many of the surrounding farms and land. Most of the building was burnt down in 1916, leaving only the service wing and walled garden. The former was eventually pulled down when the new Trefnanney Farm was built.

In the gardens of a previous house which stood on the site there were two bronze statues of Hercules and Atlas. It was said that these 'being naked, caused great offence to women and children passing down the road.'

Both this house and the medieval hall at Pontyscowrhyd are featured in a fascinating book, *The Lost Houses of Wales* by Thomas Lloyd.

In the early part of the century it was all dairy farming around Trefnanney and herds of Shorthorns, Herefords and British Friesians plodded into the milking sheds morning and evening, with a slap and a curse from the farm worker. Shining milk churns on a stand by the gate, as late as 1976, were collected each morning by lorry and taken to the creamery at Four Crosses, near Oswestry. This was taken over by the Milk Marketing Board in 1936, but is still famous for its Cheshire and Caerphilly cheeses.

More recently many farmers have turned to sheep and fatstock or pigs. There are also one or two poultry units. Many hedges have been taken out to make larger fields and farms are producing more silage to combat the inclement weather.

There is no church or chapel in Trefnanney. Some folk go to Meifod church, the origins of which go back many centuries, some go to Salem (Welsh Presbyterian) and some to Geufford chapel (English Presbyterian). This chapel was built in 1870 on the site of an older one.

Geufford means 'deep ditch', taking its name from the ditch nearby which is said to have been worn down by the feet of mules carrying iron ore from Llangynog to Pool Quay, from where it went by river to the Ironbridge foundries in Shropshire.

Many families with names such as Breeze, Francis, Pearce, Peate and Pryce have been in the area for up to 400 years.

Although more English is spoken than in the last century, many people are still Welsh-speaking, as can be heard in the nearby market town of Welshpool.

176

Tregynon

Tregynon lies in a sleepy hollow just north of Newtown on the Llanfair Caereinion road. Travellers frequently miss it, because it is not signposted until one is almost there.

But the Knights Templar of St John found it in the 12th century! They established a cell here where travellers, about to cross wild, inhospitable country, could stay and rest.

The Celtic St Cynon and his followers also found it in the 12th century and built a church. It stands today, a fine building restored in the 18th century, still a focal point in the village and lovingly cared for both inside and out by its parishioners.

The church contains memorials to the well-known people of the parish, in particular the Blayneys of Gregynog.

In the time of the Blayneys, and subsequent owners, Gregynog was a large estate, but now only the impressive black and white mansion with its extensive grounds and woodlands remains, the property of the University of Wales.

The previous owners, the Misses Davies of Llandinam, provided employment for a number of people from the village and had much influence locally. It was said that all their male employees had fine singing voices, and were members of the famous Gregynog choir. A few people worked in the private printing press which the ladies owned. Tregynon still has a lady bookbinder who worked and learned her skills there.

The ladies of Gregynog hated the 'demon drink' and caused the local pub – The Dragon – to be closed, so that their employees would not be led astray. The building stands on the crossroads and is still called The Temperance.

Until the 1950s Tregynon was a self-contained village with a larger population. It possessed a bakery, a butcher's shop and a tailoring business. The tailor also sold men's clothing and boots and shoes.

The local postmen travelled mainly on foot and conveyed the latest news and other useful information round the parish. This service, known as The Grapevine, was valued, especially by the farms and scattered houses.

Church and chapel alike were well supported. At Harvest Festival both places would be filled to capacity. It was said the back pew in church was always occupied by the farm lads who sang their own version of a famous harvest hymn – 'All is safely gathered in, Except Neuaddlwyd and Tyn-y-Bryn', those two farms being tardy harvesters!

But times changed soon after the Second World War, farming became mechanised and there were fewer jobs to be had on the land and fewer still in Newtown. There was a decline in population all round the area. Then the Mid-Wales Development Board was set up. They in time brought factories and workers to Newtown and so rural depopulation was stemmed.

Slowly, but surely, life changed once more in Tregynon. Just as the planners predicted, it became a dormitory village for Newtown. New housing was built, people from other areas moved in, some to retire, others to work in Newtown. The village had a new lease of life, for with new people came new talents, interests and ideas. The Post Bus has replaced the old bus service. The village shop has been developed and the post office restored as a full time service, all thanks to a newcomer to the village.

Trewern 🌿

Trewern means township of the alders or swamp. The village is situated two miles from the English border, and is highly populated, with farmhouses, cottages and a housing estate. It lies in the valley of the river Severn, called Sabrina by the Romans and Hafren by the Welsh. On its meanderings to the

Trewern Hall

Bristol Channel the river forms ox-bows, an ox-bow being an exaggerated curve which nearly forms an island. One of these runs through Trewern. The river floods regularly, depositing rich soil on the fields on its way.

The Breidden Hills – named Breidden, Cefn y Castell and Moel y Golfa, and the Long Mountain, or Cefn Digoll, overlook the village. The nearest of these, Moel y Golfa – Bald or Stony Hill – shelters the village. It rises to 1,324 ft and is volcanic, while the Long Mountain rises to 1,300 ft.

Recent excavations on the Breiddens have revealed Bronze Age artefacts, of a much earlier date than was anticipated. Caradoc's last stand against the Romans in AD 50 is supposed to have taken place here, an eternally debatable point. On the tops of the hills are hill forts and ancient fields. In prehistoric times the valley was wet, uninhabitable and full of wild animals. Now a herd of fallow deer, escapees from Loton Park, just across the English border, roam the hillside.

179

Trinity Well, one of many so called, which still supplies water to the houses on the side of the hill, was visited in olden times by young couples plighting their troth. They would drink the water sweetened with sugar then retire to the Pheasant Inn to dance to the music of a fiddler. Older people also used to pledge their continued love, no doubt not to be left out of the festivities!

At the top of Moel y Golfa is a monument built by gipsies in memory of their leader. The monument is made of Cornish granite, the hardest granite in Britain.

Buzzards are seen flying high, kestrels and cormorants range over the valley. Three rare plants grow on the hills, rock cinquefoil, spiked speedwell and a sticky catchfly, all highly protected. Dragonflies have been photographed over a pool. These areas were common land until the Enclosure Act of 1811.

Through the area passes the A458 trunk road, built in the early 19th century. This carries a great volume of traffic, heavy lorries during the week and visitors to the sea at weekends. There are plans to build a new road from Middletown to Buttington, marring this beautiful valley.

From Middletown, on the way down Golfa Bank, is a small Victorian chapel, daughter to Buttington church. Trewern House, a timbered farmhouse restored by the present owners, is further along, followed by Maesfron, circa 1829, behind which lies Trewern Old Post Office. Once the Pheasant Inn, this is now a private dwelling, as the post office no longer functions. Below the hill is the post-war housing estate, Pentre Gwyn – 'white hamlet' – consisting of 49 houses and two bungalows.

In the valley is Llwyn Melyn, a medieval farmhouse with two cruck roof trusses, the oldest house in the area. Further along is Trewern Hall, circa 1560. This house was protected by an argae, or earth bank, from the floods. Over the passage of time it has been neglected causing the house to be flooded, and, as a consequence, to drop by 18 inches. In 1985 half of the house was restored by raising it to the right level and replacing the rotten beams with green oak. The other half is due to be restored soon. Middle Heldre farm is also a listed building, in fact many local houses, particularly farms, are centuries old.

Farming in the valley is arable and sheep and cattle rearing, dairy farming having largely died out. Employment is agricultural, with some work at Buttington brickworks, though many people travel to Welshpool or Shrewsbury to work. A large percentage of the residents are local, though many cottages have been modernised and new bungalows built since the Second World War.

Trewern has a new school built in 1953 to replace the Victorian schools of Trewern, Buttington and Pool Quay, as well as latterly of Middletown. The school is attractively situated, giving the children idyllic surroundings with a tree-lined drive and roses and daffodils in season.

Incorporated in the school is the community centre, comprising a large hall, sports room and functions room. The hall is acoustically good, and Buttington and District Amateur Operatic Society stages productions there every year.

Finally, in Trewern is a small area called Cefn, meaning ridge. The soil contains many fossils, the clay being used by the brickworks. A few modernised cottages, one an old shop, and three new bungalows lie at Cefn, also a Methodist church, circa 1881.

Tylwch 🦢

Tylwch lies where two districts, Montgomery and Radnor, meet, as well as three parishes, Llangurig, Llandinam and St Harmon. The river Dulas flows through the valley bottom, meandering over its rocky bed.

Once, the railway station was the hub of the community. Everyone went to meet the train. There was a stationmaster and two porters until the late 1920s. Farmers would have a wagon of lime or coal delivered to the siding and take it home by horse and cart. Lead from the mines around also came to the station and was taken away by goods wagon. But in 1962 Beeching's 'axe' fell on the railway and the station was closed. It had won first prize for some years for being the best kept station between Moat Lane and Builth on the Cambrian Railway. At the end of the 19th century there was an accident in the station when a train taking a church trip from St Harmon ran into a stationary one. One young woman was killed.

Below the station there was a mill where farmers took their wheat to be ground into flour to make bread for their families. The bread was baked in big ovens in the kitchens, heated red and white-hot with wood. They grew barley to fatten pigs, which every householder kept, and killed for their family.

Other local industries were based at the woollen mill and the tannery. The latter lasted longer than the woollen or corn mills, finishing around 1920. Around the time of the First World War, Frank Williams employed four men making clogs.

The tavern used to be at the Brook House, where a blacksmith had his forge, but when it moved over the border into Montgomeryshire it failed to get a licence, because Llandinam parish was temperance!

The curate for the little church of Banhadlog, just over the hill, lived at the vicarage, now named Bronygraig.

Legend says that Prince Llewelyn rode his horse with its shoes on backwards across the hill of Cwmfron, to mislead the enemy. Nearby, there is a house called Ty Llewelyn, where he is supposed to have stayed.

Today the people are mostly farmers. The tractor and its

different implements has replaced the shire horses. Crops are gathered as silage or hay, in bales. No one sows or harvests grain any more. Sheep are to be seen everywhere and the red and white Hereford cattle have been replaced by the Charolais.

An artist, a hairdresser and a photographer who also makes cameras, work in the area.

In February 1970 a public inquiry was held in Llanidloes about the proposed building of a dam on the river. Supported by Lord Hooson, the villagers won the day, thanks to the community spirit of the people.

Welshpool 🌿

Welshpool (Y Trallwm, to be correct) is a border town with the heart of a village, situated amongst the foothills of the Severn valley. Its name, it is said, derives from the Llyn-du Pool in Powis Castle park. Old Leland, writing in the 16th century says 'Betwixt the town and Castell Coch (Powis Castle) is a pretty llyn or pool, whereof the town takes its name'. The town received its first charter in 1263 from Griffith ap Wenwynwyn, Prince of Powys. It was known as Poole, but after the Municipal Corporation Act in 1835 the prefix 'Welsh' was added to distinguish it from Poole in Dorset.

One of the dominant landmarks of Welshpool is Powis Castle, which dates back to the 13th century. The castle is conspicuous because of the red sandstone out of which it is built. It has important historical connections with Clive of India, and apart from its magnificent gardens, the castle now houses an exhibition of the spoils of war that Clive brought back. The grounds were renovated by Capability Brown, contain oaks hundreds of years old and a Douglas fir over 160 ft high, said to be the tallest tree in Britain.

Eighteenth century octagonal cock-pit, Welshpool

Traditionally a market town, it now, like much of the rest of the Principality, relies on tourism to an increasing degree. In this respect the town is well served by the attraction of the narrow gauge railway which was first opened in 1903. It has a gauge of 2 ft 6 ins, and was originally nine miles long. It has been painstakingly restored by steam engine enthusiasts. The town also has one of the few well-preserved octagonal cockpits. It dates from the 18th century, and is a relic of more callous days when cock-fighting was a popular sport. The old Shropshire Union Canal passes through the town and lapsed into disuse for many years, but there are movements afoot to restore it to its former glory.

In the midst of an area which boasts many fine examples of Tudor and Georgian architecture, one or two merit special mention. The Prentice Traders is one, formerly 'The Sun in Armour', which is a half-timbered Tudor building. The other is Grace Evans' Cottage, which is situated near the chancel of St Mary's parish church. This black and white cottage was once the home of the courageous maid, Grace Evans, who assisted Lady Nithsdale – daughter of the Earl of Powis – to rescue her husband, the Jacobite leader, from the Tower of London in 1716 on the eve of his execution. He had been sentenced to death for his complicity in the 1715 rebellion. 'My dear Evans', as Lady Nithsdale always called her, was given the cottage in gratitude.

The town is well represented by two Anglican churches, a modern Roman Catholic church and seven Nonconformist churches. About ten yards from the south porch of St Mary's church is the great glacial boulder stone well which is said to have been used by the Druids as an altar upon which offerings were made. Bishop Morgan, who translated the Bible into Welsh, was vicar of Welshpool from 1575 to 1578.

There is still a strong dependence on agriculture, as evidenced by the largest weekly one-day sheep sale in Europe, which has the effect of transforming the calm and quietness of Welshpool on a Monday into an extremely busy town, with the influx of the farming community from outlying districts. Welshpool also possesses a modern industrial estate. This was started initially by private enterprise but was then encouraged by Mid Wales Development. The historical connection with printing continues with at least four high-class printing firms, and one originating house, located in and around the town producing work for the international market.

A two day Festival of Transport takes place in July and the County Agricultural Show is held earlier in the year.

The long-heralded talk of a bypass for Welshpool is nearing reality, and its effect on the town, whether contentious or otherwise, has yet to be evidenced but, hopefully, the tourists passing through Welshpool on their way to the Welsh Coast during the summer will no longer have to suffer long traffic delays.

The Wern & Burgedin 🌿

The Wern is situated nearly three miles north-east of Guilsfield and is a hamlet of scattered farms and cottages crossed by narrow, winding lanes, public footpaths, the Guilsfield brook and the Shropshire Union Canal (now usually referred to as the Montgomery Canal).

Burgedin is not so much a hamlet as a name given to several features in this area – a farm (Burgedin Hall), a shop (Burgedin Shop – not in operation since about 1960, but marked on the OS map) and Burgedin Lock on the canal.

As in other parts of Britain the canal has long been disused for commercial purposes, but its history is an interesting one. Its main purpose in this area was to carry and distribute limestone for agricultural purposes from Llanymynech Hill, about five miles away. The lime required by the farmers was slaked lime, produced in kilns, but as this was an exceedingly volatile cargo to carry, turning caustic on contact with the water in a leaking canal boat, numerous kilns were built along the full length of the canal. The remains of two of these kilns can be seen in a knacker's yard about a mile south-west of Burgedin Hall, beside the Guilsfield arm of the canal. This is an interesting offshoot of the canal, which served farmers between Burgedin Lock and Guilsfield. Due to its low-key management since its decline, a very diverse flora and fauna has become established here. It also boasts the deepest cutting on the waterway (Deep Cutting), which has been colonised by a community of badgers, as well as many other animals, birds and plants of interest to naturalists and towpath walkers alike.

Most canals were built over the watershed between rivers, and were therefore lowest at either end, but the Montgomery Canal is an exception to the rule, flowing down from Newtown to The Wern and up again towards Ellesmere, the lowest point occurring at The Wern. Today, the picnic area at Red Bridge is a popular spot with visitors, who can fish, stroll, birdwatch or read of the spot's former importance – a drainage leat cut to take excess water back to the Severn was put to good use driving a mill. The foundations of this are clearly visible, along with the mill pool and sluice arrangement. There was also a good source of puddling clay here, which was exploited from the early days of the canal right up to 1984, for waterproofing the canal bed. The Wern Clay Pit sign is still in place at the roadside. Cattle were driven up and down the clay-lined canal bed to 'puddle' the clay. Maps of the early 20th century show a brick and tile works here too, but this was a short-lived enterprise.

Today little evidence remains of these former activities, and nature has taken over again. The clay pits have been designated a nature reserve, and several lagoons have been formed, fed by the canal overflow. It is hoped that the canal will shortly be restored to a navigable standard, and the lagoons are designed to support the rare plant species for which the canal is particularly valuable, but which would be much reduced by repeated 'traffic' on the waterway.

The locks at Burgedin are being restored again, and the interesting lock-house surviving alongside the canal, together with its two stalls (for the barge horses) and pig-sties, may well be inhabited again shortly. Meanwhile the swans on the river reflect the grace and tranquillity of the area.

Bridge over the Vyrnwy, Llansantffraid

Index

Aberbechan 9
Abercegir (see Darowen) 51
Aberglesyrch (see Ceinws) 44
Aberhafesp 10
Aberhosan 13
Aberllefenni (see Ceinws) 44
Abermule 15
Achor (see Ceinws) 44
Adfa 19
Alberbury (see Coedway) 49
Arddleen 19

Bausley (see Coedway) 49
Belan 21
Berriew 24
Bethel (see Aberhafesp) 10
Bettws Cedewain 27
Beulah 31
Blackhall (see Kerry) 74
Blaenglyn (see Beulah) 31
Bont Dolgadfan (see
    Llanbrynmair) 80
Bontfaen (see Forge) 63
Brithdir (see Belan) 21
Brooks 32
Bumbletown (see Middletown)
    141
Burgedin (see The Wern) 186
Buttington 33
Bwlch-y-Cibau 34
Bwlchffrido (see Aberhafesp) 10

Caersws 36
Carno 38
Castle Caereinion 40

Cefn Coch 43
Ceinws 44
Churchstoke 48
Coedway 49
Crew Green (see Coedway) 49
Criggion (see Coedway) 49
Cwm Bychan (see Darowen) 51
Cyfronydd (see Castle
    Caereinion) 40

Darowen 51
Derwen (see Guilsfield) 68
Derwenlas 54
Deytheur (see Penrhos) 158
Dolanog 56
Dolfor 58
Dylife 60

Esgairgeiliog (see Ceinws) 44
Esgairgoch (see Staylittle) 171

Ffynnonycorn (see Llanwnog)
    125
Forden 61
Forge 63
The Fron 65
Four Crosses 66

Geuffordd (see Guilsfield) 68
Glantwymyn (see Aberhosan) 13
The Green (see New Mills) 149
Groes Ilwyd (see Guilsfield) 68
Guilsfield 68
Guilsfield Within (see Guilsfield)
    68

Guilsfield Without (see
    Guildsfield) 68

Haimwood (see Llandrinio) 88
Halfway Fron (see The Fron) 65
Hillcrest (see Aberhafesp) 10
Hyssington 72

Kerry 74

Leighton 78
Llanbrynmair 80
Llandinam 85
Llandrinio 88
Llandysilio (see Four Crosses) 66
Llandyssil 90
Llanfair Caereinion 92
Llanfechain 95
Llanfihangel yng Ngwynfa 98
Llanfyllin 100
Llangadfan (see Llwydiarth) 132
Llangurig 102
Llangynog 105
Llangynyw 107
Llanidloes 109
Llanllugan (see Adfa) 19
Llanllwchaiarn 113
Llanmerewig 114
Llanrhaeadr-ym-Mochnant 115
Llansantffraid-ym-Mechain 118
Llanwddyn 121
Llanwnog 125
Llanwrin 127
Llanymynech 129
Llidiartywaen (see Newchapel)
    151
Llwydiarth 132
Llwynderw (see Belan) 21
Llynebyr (see Trefeglwys) 172

Machynlleth 136

Maesmawr (see Guilsfield) 68
Manafon (see New Mills) 149
Mathafarn (see Llanwrin) 127
Mathrafal (see Meifod) 138
Meifod 138
Melinygloch (see Aberhafesp) 10
Melverley (see Coedway) 49
Middletown 141
Mochdre 144
Montgomery 146

Nelly Andrews Green (see
    Buttington) 33
New Mills 149
Newchapel 151
Newtown 153

Oakley Park (see Newchapel) 151

Pandy (see Llanbrynmair) 80
Pant (see Llanymynech) 129
Pantybeni (see Carno) 38
Penegoes 156
Penfforddlas (see Staylittle) 171
Pennant 157
Penrhos 158
Penstrowed 160
Pentre (see Aberhafesp) 10
Penybontfawr 162
Penygreen (see Llanidloes) 109
Pontllogel (see Llwydiarth) 132
Pont Robert 166

Rhiwdyfeity (see Staylittle) 171
Rhydyfelin (see Aberhafesp) 10

Sarn 169
Sarnau (see Penrhos) 158
Staylittle 171
Stepaside (see Mochdre) 144

191

Sylvaen (see Castle Caereinion) 40

Tafolwern (see Llanbrynmair) 80
Talerddig (see Carno) 38
Tal y Wern (see Darowen) 51
Trefeglwys 172
Trefnanney 174

Tregynon 177
Trelystan (see Leighton) 78
Trewern 178
Ty Brith (see Carno) 38
Tylwch 181

Welshpool 183
The Wern 186